Quantifying Research Integrity

Synthesis Lectures on Information Concepts, Retrieval, and Services

Editor

Gary Marchionini, *University of North Carolina at Chapel Hill*

Synthesis Lectures on Information Concepts, Retrieval, and Services publishes short books on topics pertaining to information science and applications of technology to information discovery, production, distribution, and management. Potential topics include: data models, indexing theory and algorithms, classification, information architecture, information economics, privacy and identity, scholarly communication, bibliometrics and webometrics, personal information management, human information behavior, digital libraries, archives and preservation, cultural informatics, information retrieval evaluation, data fusion, relevance feedback, recommendation systems, question answering, natural language processing for retrieval, text summarization, multimedia retrieval, multilingual retrieval, and exploratory search.

Learning from Multiple Social Networks
Liqiang Nie, Xuemeng Song, and Tat-Seng Chua
2016

Scholarly Collaboration on the Academic Social Web
Daqing He and Wei Jeng
2016

Scalability Challenges in Web Search Engines
B. Barla Cambazoglu and Ricardo Baeza-Yates
2015

Social Informatics Evolving
Pnina Fichman, Madelyn R. Sanfilippo, and Howard Rosenbaum
2015

On the Efficient Determination of Most Near Neighbors: Horseshoes, Hand Grenades,
Web Search and Other Situations When Close Is Close Enough, Second Edition
Mark S. Manasse
2015

Building a Better World with Our Information: The Future of Personal Information
Management, Part 3
William Jones
2015

Click Models for Web Search
Aleksandr Chuklin, Ilya Markov, and Maarten de Rijke
2015

Information Communication
Feicheng Ma
2015

Social Media and Library Services
Lorri Mon
2015

Analysis and Visualization of Citation Networks
Dangzhi Zhao and Andreas Strotmann
2015

The Taxobook: Applications, Implementation, and Integration in Search: Part 3 of a 3-Part
Series
Marjorie M.K. Hlava
2014

The Taxobook: Principles and Practices of Building Taxonomies, Part 2 of a 3-Part Series
Marjorie M.K. Hlava
2014

Measuring User Engagement
Mounia Lalmas, Heather O'Brien, and Elad Yom-Tov
2014

The Taxobook: History, Theories, and Concepts of Knowledge Organization, Part 1 of a
3-Part Series
Marjorie M.K. Hlava
2014

Children's Internet Search: Using Roles to Understand Children's Search Behavior
Elizabeth Foss and Allison Druin
2014

Digital Library Technologies: Complex Objects, Annotation, Ontologies, Classification,
Extraction, and Security
Edward A. Fox and Ricardo da Silva Torres
2014

Digital Libraries Applications: CBIR, Education, Social Networks, eScience/Simulation,
and GIS
Edward A. Fox and Jonathan P. Leidig
2014

Information and Human Values
Kenneth R. Fleischmann
2013

Multiculturalism and Information and Communication Technology
Pnina Fichman and Madelyn R. Sanfilippo
2013

Transforming Technologies to Manage Our Information: The Future of Personal
Information Management, Part II
William Jones
2013

Designing for Digital Reading
Jennifer Pearson, George Buchanan, and Harold Thimbleby
2013

Information Retrieval Models: Foundations and Relationships
Thomas Roelleke
2013

Key Issues Regarding Digital Libraries: Evaluation and Integration
Rao Shen, Marcos André Gonçalves, and Edward A. Fox
2013

Visual Information Retrieval using Java and LIRE
Mathias Lux and Oge Marques
2013

On the Efficient Determination of Most Near Neighbors: Horseshoes, Hand Grenades,
Web Search and Other Situations When Close is Close Enough
Mark S. Manasse
2012

The Answer Machine
Susan E. Feldman
2012

Theoretical Foundations for Digital Libraries: The 5S (Societies, Scenarios, Spaces,
Structures, Streams) Approach
Edward A. Fox, Marcos André Gonçalves, and Rao Shen
2012

The Future of Personal Information Management, Part I: Our Information, Always and
Forever
William Jones
2012

Search User Interface Design
Max L. Wilson
2011

Information Retrieval Evaluation
Donna Harman
2011

Knowledge Management (KM) Processes in Organizations: Theoretical Foundations and
Practice
Claire R. McInerney and Michael E. D. Koenig
2011

Search-Based Applications: At the Confluence of Search and Database Technologies
Gregory Grefenstette and Laura Wilber
2010

Information Concepts: From Books to Cyberspace Identities
Gary Marchionini
2010

Quantifying Research Integrity

Michael Seadle

ISBN: 978-3-031-01178-8   paperback
ISBN: 978-3-031-02306-4   ebook

DOI 10.1007/978-3-031-02306-4

A Publication in the Springer series
SYNTHESIS LECTURES ON INFORMATION CONCEPTS, RETRIEVAL, AND SERVICES

Lecture #53
Series Editor: Gary Marchionini, *University of North Carolina at Chapel Hill*
Series ISSN
Print 1947-945X   Electronic 1947-9468

Quantifying Research Integrity

Michael Seadle
Humboldt-Universität zu Berlin

SYNTHESIS LECTURES ON INFORMATION CONCEPTS, RETRIEVAL, AND SERVICES #53

ABSTRACT

Institutions typically treat research integrity violations as black and white, right or wrong. The result is that the wide range of grayscale nuances that separate accident, carelessness, and bad practice from deliberate fraud and malpractice often get lost. This lecture looks at how to quantify the grayscale range in three kinds of research integrity violations: plagiarism, data falsification, and image manipulation.

Quantification works best with plagiarism, because the essential one-to-one matching algorithms are well known and established tools for detecting when matches exist. Questions remain, however, of how many matching words of what kind in what location in which discipline constitute reasonable suspicion of fraudulent intent. Different disciplines take different perspectives on quantity and location. Quantification is harder with data falsification, because the original data are often not available, and because experimental replication remains surprisingly difficult. The same is true with image manipulation, where tools exist for detecting certain kinds of manipulations, but where the tools are also easily defeated.

This lecture looks at how to prevent violations of research integrity from a pragmatic viewpoint, and at what steps can institutions and publishers take to discourage problems beyond the usual ethical admonitions. There are no simple answers, but two measures can help: the systematic use of detection tools and requiring original data and images. These alone do not suffice, but they represent a start.

The scholarly community needs a better awareness of the complexity of research integrity decisions. Only an open and wide-spread international discussion can bring about a consensus on where the boundary lines are and when grayscale problems shade into black. One goal of this work is to move that discussion forward.

KEYWORDS

research integrity, plagiarism, data falsification, image manipulation, grayscale decisions, research fraud, detection tools, plagiarism tools, forensic droplets, Retraction Watch, Office of Research Integrity, HEADT Centre

To my wife Joan

Contents

xvi

Preface

Research integrity problems are nothing new.[1] While student misconduct is an important and much discussed issue, this lecture focuses on integrity issues involving the scientific and scholarly record. Frauds, mistakes, and retractions undermine the credibility of both the sciences and the humanities. Today, for example, elements of the popular press are skeptical about atmospheric change and global warming because they doubt the reliability of the theories and data that undergird the claims. Skeptics can point to retractions as evidence that science is flawed. The need for discovering and preventing research malpractice grows as the quantity of publication grows.

Retractions are in themselves not bad, because they are evidence of a self-policing process for the scholarly record. Nonetheless a different kind of danger exists when self-policing becomes a vigilante process with no clear rules or limits. As chair of my university's Commission on Research Malpractice,[2] I have encountered a wide range of accusations, some based on personal animus, some based on unrealistic standards of perfection, and many where the commission itself had to establish rules. The problem is that our scholarly measures for research integrity lack precision. The goal of this lecture is to suggest more accurate and more appropriate metrics to improve the self-policing process. I choose the term "quantification" for this because the goal is to approach a more formal and more mathematical accuracy in making judgments, even though missing information and unclear circumstances often reduce actual quantification to no more than a goal.

This work can also be read as a form of history of science that looks at the flaws and failings of the scholarly process. As scholars we often wish to believe that we create knowledge by building on discoveries from the past, but it may be more realistic to add that the discovery process also involves exposing frauds, mistakes, and other forms of intentional and unintentional error. Sometimes this is viewed critically, because people forget that scientists are mere humans working at a particular time in a particular place, as Steven Shapin explains in "Lowering the tone in the history of science" [Shapin, 2010]. The examples in this lecture come mostly from recent years, in part because new cases keep coming to light, but also to show how current the problem is. This lecture does not speculate about why well-trained scholars engage in malpractice. The reasons are too complex for simple answers like greed or peer pressure or cultural tolerance. It would take a more extensive work to gain a real understanding of the full range of social, psychological, and cultural factors involved in research integrity violations.

The risk in writing any lecture about research integrity issue is that the author must be absolutely scrupulous. This is particularly true in the area of plagiarism. Some plagiarism hunters regard paraphrasing even with a proper reference as a violation. For that reason I have chosen to

---

[1] See the literature review in Chapter 2.
[2] In German: Kommission zur Überprüfung von Vorwürfen wissenschaftlichen Fehlverhaltens.

quote directly from sources, rather than to summarize or paraphrase the information they provide. This also has the benefit of letting readers judge the sources for themselves.

Confidentiality and anonymity are important issues for any commission investigating research integrity cases, because the mere suggestion of malpractice can destroy careers. In this work I have used only cases where the accusations are publicly available. For cases that are very current and potentially undecided, I have deliberately left out the full names and used only abbreviations. Links in the references do, however, point to the actual accusations, which include the names of those involved. This offers a modest if imperfect balance between transparency and confidentiality. Readers who genuinely want to get at the names in publicly available materials may do so, but they must make an extra effort. One option would be to write a purely theoretical work about how research integrity issues should be measured, but that would perpetuate the existing tendency toward oversimplification. The messy empirical details of the cases matter in understanding how and how well quantification works.

Michael Seadle
Berlin, December 2016

Acknowledgments

First and foremost I would like to acknowledge the contributions of my wife, Prof. Dr. Joan Luft, for her suggestions, proofreading, and loving support. I could not have completed this work without her.

I would also like to thank my staff, Melanie Rügenhagen, Dr. Thorsten Beck, Ulrike Stöckel, and Stephanie van de Sandt for their encouragement and support.

My university colleagues, especially Prof. Dr. Elke Greifeneder and Prof. Dr. Vivien Petras, have given advice and picked up tasks that I could not get done. Our Vice-President for Research, Prof. Dr. Peter Frensch, also deserves credit for the many discussions we had about research integrity issues. Many other colleagues and students who are too numerous to name individually should be thanked for conversations and idea as well.

I would like to thank Gobinda Chowdhury, Lynn Silipigni Connaway, and John Budd for their helpful comments and suggestions.

Finally I would like to thank Elsevier for funding the Humboldt Elsevier Advanced Data and Text Centre, which made part of this research possible. And I want to recognize Humboldt-Universität zu Berlin for providing an intellectual atmosphere in keeping with the traditions Hegel, Planck, Einstein, and other notable scholars.

Michael Seadle
Berlin, December 2016

CHAPTER 1

Introduction

1.1 OVERVIEW

Publishers, editors, and scholars tend to think of research integrity as a black and white binary choice: researchers have violated integrity or they have not. This is too simple and does not reflect the real world. A simple metaphor helps to explain this. When scanning a full-color photograph, a one-bit (black and white) digital rendering strips all subtlety from the original. A photograph with many soft shades may become almost unrecognizable in a purely black-and-white scan, and the same level of distortion can occur with an overly simplistic approach to research integrity. Assessing research integrity violations needs to involve a grayscale range that distinguishes among the types of possible violations. Just as the scanning process involves categorizing—and measuring—the differences between shades, a systematic approach to research integrity should involve measuring the amount of deviation between suspected problems and an expected ideal.

Most actual cases involve complex trade-offs and judgments in an attempt to understand the author's intention. In mathematical terms, concepts like "true" and "original" are limits that researchers can approach but can never completely reach. No scholarly research is or should be totally original because scholarship in the natural sciences, as in the social sciences and humanities, explicitly builds on previous work, and the truth of a claim or of a set of data or of an image depends in part on the social acceptance of the circumstances of their origin.[1] It is a principle of the natural sciences today that discoveries build on past works. In this context originality represents a modest step, an increment, toward a new level of "truth." Investigations of research integrity need to measure the asymptotic distance between the curve of reality and an unreachable ideal. The goal of this monograph is to establish measurement strategies to create a grayscale range for three common types of research integrity issues: plagiarism, data falsification, and image manipulation.

1.2 CONTEXT

Context matters, and the standards for research integrity are not the same in different disciplines, in part because of different ideas of what matters in a scholarly work. In broad terms the sciences care more about whether the data in a scholarly work leads to a valid and reproducible conclusion, and show some flexibility about whether the text contains standard phrases that can be found in other works, while the humanities care strongly about the originality of the language. There are shades of variation within each discipline, and variations across countries and cultures. This lecture

---

[1]Social acceptance is especially a factor in the humanities.

cannot sample more than a few disciplines across the broad subject spectrum, and this will focus on examples from universities in northern Europe and North America, since that is the world the author knows.

The disciplines themselves are a driving force in how scholars conceptualize research integrity. As Abbott [2001] writes:

> "And being an academic means, willy-nilly, being a member of a discipline. ... Other disciplinary functions are cultural rather than social structural. The first of these is the Geertzian function of providing academics with a general conception of intellectual existence, a conception of the proper units of knowledge."

The "proper units of knowledge" are exactly the means by which members of a discipline measure violations against their standards for integrity. For older disciplines, these units tend to be clearer than for newer ones. Historians, for example, react strongly not only against forged texts (data falsification) but against texts taken out of context (which is a form of data manipulation). A younger discipline like information science may have less of a consensus about when data is taken out of context, because the boundaries are still broader and more open.

1.3   TIME

Time matters as well, not only because the disciplines and their boundaries change over time, but because the standards for acceptable research also change. One of the clearest examples of change in a discipline in recent decades occurred in cultural anthropology (often called social anthropology in the UK and ethnography in Germany). When Clifford Geertz was a doctoral student and for a long time afterward, the norm among Anglo-American anthropologists was to send students to remote parts of the world to get experience with different cultures. Geertz himself went to Indonesia and later to Morocco. These were not primitive cultures of the sort that Claude Lévi-Strauss investigated, but were technologically less advanced and less connected to Western legal systems. This meant that interviews and observation could be done with impunity and without any except an implicit permission.

By the time that Bonnie Nardi and Vicki O'Day did their observations of libraries in the late 1990s, anthropologists had changed their focus to our contemporary society. Getting permission from the people being observed increasingly became an issue, especially after many universities set up review boards to decide whether the research should be allowed. This changed the nature of data collection and the definition of what data are legitimate. Ethnographic interviews once required note taking, and the quality of that evidence depended on the quality of the notes. Today it has become normal to record interviews, sometimes even to do a video-recording. This has changed expectations about accuracy and sometimes calls into question the work of researchers who use notes only, even in circumstances where recording is not possible.

Looking further back in time, instances of what might today be called research integrity problems touch even famous and highly respectable scholars. Zeldin [1979] writes:

"Michelet contrasted aristocratic England, owned by 32,000 rich men who got others to work for them, with democratic France, where the land was shared out between 15 or 20 million peasants who cultivated it themselves. These figures were quite mythical …" [p. 143]

"Michelet got this figure [peasant landowners] out of his own head. He could not have got it from anywhere else, because the number of landowners was unknown in his day, and remained unknown throughout this period. The statistics the government collected were incapable of revealing the facts because they were compiled from taxation returns made for other purposes." [p. 148]

Zeldin may just be speculating that Michelet made up the numbers, but such an accusation would have a devastating effect if Michelet were alive today. As it is, few are aware of the issue. The numbers do not undermine the whole of his contribution, and represent almost a puzzle about why he would invent the details.

Instances of data falsification are harder to find among chemists and physicists, since the reproducibility of results has long been a hallmark of those fields and offers a concrete benchmark. The 1989 experiments that appeared to be evidence for cold fusion were quickly discounted, and there is no clear evidence that the scientists involved intended fraud, only that their interpretation of the data was flawed. Within the biological sciences more cases of questionable data exist, in particular during the 19th and 20th century when society broadly accepted certain kinds of data as a basis for claiming significant racial differences. In many of these cases the data themselves may have been accurate, but the context in which they were used and the conclusions scientists drew from them are now discounted. Data falsification is not merely about the manufacture of data, but also about manipulating them in a context that leads to false conclusions. Again this is a gray-zone issue that seems as obviously problematic today as it seemed plainly plausible in previous centuries to people who had a predisposition to believe the results.

1.4   IMAGES

Paintings and drawings have always had an interpretative nature, even when scientists in past centuries tried to make them as accurate as possible (some biologists still prefer drawings today).[2] The invention of the daguerreotype process in the 1830s and the cameras that followed gave the impression of a perfectly accurate image. The illusion was soon shattered, as Sontag [1977] writes:

"…in the mid-1840s a German photographer invented the first technique for retouching the negative. His two versions of the same portrait—one retouched, the other not—astounded crowds at the Exposition Universelle held in Paris in 1855 (the second world fair, and the first with a photography exhibit). The news that the camera could lie made getting photographed much more popular." [p. 86]

---

[2]For example, see Beck [2016], pp. 77–79.

The most famous examples of image manipulation came from the dictatorships of the 1930s. When Stalin purged a member of his Politburo, he also had them removed from official photographs, as if they had never existed. Photographs were relatively rarely published in the scholarly literature until the later twentieth century, simply because the cost of reproducing a photograph on paper was high when done with a quality sufficient for scholarly purposes.

Manipulating a chemical negative to produce an altered photograph often required talent and training that most amateur photographers, including scientists, lacked. Some forms of manipulation were comparatively easy, such as cropping an image to leave out unwanted parts along the edges, or making the image lighter or darker. The scope for fraud with these techniques was limited, even for someone who already had a darkroom, the right chemicals, and sufficient time. Scientific photos in the era of chemical film tended to use silver halide film that produced a black and white (actually grayscale) image, partly because the colors in color film tended to deteriorate over time, but mainly because printing color photographs was prohibitively expensive.

Digital cameras changed the situation once the quality became competitive with chemical photography. Photoshop appeared on the market in 1990 and GIMP (GNU Image Manipulation Program) five years later. This software made alterations in digital images that took real expertise in a darkroom almost trivially easy, including copying (inserting) and erasing content. At the same time digital processes made including images in print publications far less costly than before. As more and more of the scholarly literature became primarily digital, especially in the natural sciences, the inclusion of images became common, even sometimes expected. It is not fair to say that Photoshop and GIMP opened the door to potential fraud, but they did make fraud easier, and they raised questions about where the legitimate boundaries of manipulation were in different disciplines.

This introduction has offered a quick historical overview of some of the key research integrity issues that face the scholarly world today. The following chapters will look more specifically at plagiarism, data falsification, and image manipulation. First, however, a look at the current literature and tools will help the reader to understand the state of the art of research integrity research.

CHAPTER 2

State of the Art

2.1 INTRODUCTION

The number of articles written about research integrity issues reaches into the tens of thousands since the year 2000. A quick search for "plagiarism" on Google Scholar (excluding citations) gives about 68,000 hits, a search for "research integrity" gets 16,700 hits, "scientific misconduct" gets about 8,000 hits, "image manipulation" gets 16,000 hits, and a search for "data falsification" and "research" gets 2,000 hits.[1] Google Scholar is by no means a completely reliable indicator, but it serves to give the relative magnitude. A search for "Plagiat" (the word for plagiarism in German and French) gives 16,000 hits. The issue is international, and it is widespread.

Research integrity problems cross disciplinary boundaries too, and the issue is particularly sensitive in medicine, because of the effect that false information can have on patients. As David Ploth [2014] wrote in the article "Ethics in publishing—today's epidemic":[2]

> "...some 23% of submitted material is reported to be rejected by 1 publisher because of plagiarism. The rate of retraction of published material has increased dramatically to about 800 papers per year, reflecting a 10-fold increase in retractions of published material during the past decade. ... It is a fool's game to try to beat the system with plagiarism in the present day. Publishers have incredibly powerful software search engines at nearly every journal's disposal."

The last two sentences imply a level of reliability that plagiarism-discovery tools generally do not claim, and it implies a degree of malicious intent in trying "to beat the system." One of the purposes of this lecture is to develop appropriate metrics to describe the levels of violation within the discovery process, and with these metrics to help readers and evaluators to make a more nuanced judgment about how much malicious intent (vs. sloppiness, laziness, or accident) plays a role in particular cases.

The goal of this chapter is to give a brief overview of the literature about research integrity issues, including ethics, prevention, detection tools, case studies, and replication studies. Works relating to research integrity metrics tend to focus on the external question of how large the problem is, rather than looking at individual cases to understand more precisely how to know when and where an author moves from mere sloppiness and poor judgment to deliberate falsification.

---

[1]As of 26 September 2016.

[2]As a general rule in this lecture, references to articles in the text will include the article's title, since it provides useful context information.

The latter matters particularly in legal cases, in which an author challenges a retraction, and this topic is poorly represented in the current literature.

2.2   LEGAL ISSUES

A legal issue involving copyright violation can exist any time an author copies from another without attribution, even when the copying is inadvertent and from memory, as long as the original text still has copyright protection, which is generally the case with contemporary scholarly and scientific publications. The legal questions can become complicated when they are actually brought to court, but legal cases involving plagiarism are still relatively rare. More often in the literature writers discuss ethical issues. Any serious analysis of the legal issues depends on venue and circumstances and is beyond the scope of this short lecture, but readers should be aware that legal complications exist. Universities and publishers must regularly make both a legal and financial assessment when retracting a work or withdrawing a degree for those cases where an author takes them to court. For those taking action against malpractice, a well-nuanced factual case is essential.

2.3   ETHICS

A large number of articles about research integrity issues have to do with ethics, including the legal issues involving copyright violations. For many in a broad range of fields, it is a question of right and wrong. In "Response to Diane Pecorari's 'Plagiarism in second language writing: Is it time to close the case?' " Debbie Weber-Wulff writes:

> "Many university instructors I have spoken with over the past decade have observed that L2 [second language] students plagiarize more often than their L1 [first or native language] peers. Cultural explanations are indeed often offered, and students will say, when questioned, that they didn't mean to do anything wrong. But from my perspective, it is quite irrelevant why they have plagiarized. They have simply submitted the work of others as their own and that is not acceptable." [Weber-Wulff, 2015, p. 103]

This reflects the hard-line approach in which any copying for any reason is plagiarism and is unacceptable.

Typical titles include "The road to fraud starts with a single step," by Jennifer Crocker, who was reacting to the Diederik Stapel case:

> "The well-being of science and our society requires that fraud be punished severely. But a heavy focus on fraudsters may also conveniently divert our attention from the fraudster within us all. Who cannot find places where they took a first step, or perhaps several steps, down one slippery slope or another?" [Crocker, 2011]

Crocker's concept of the first step is relevant to developing metrics, since reliable and specific metrics help scholars to become aware of when they risk plagiarism accusations. The paper on "Ethics in the authorship and publishing of scientific articles," by Shewan and Coats, suggests requiring authors to agree to an ethical statement:

"Whilst we cannot claim that this has stopped fraud the number of cases brought to our attention has begun to fall, and perhaps most importantly cases have been easier to deal with, as the authors have agreed how their cases should be handled if subsequent evidence suggests errors, omissions or misleading statements with regard to authorship, ownership or veracity of data and the correct citing of previous work." [Shewan and Coats, 2010]

Establishing an agreement about how cases should be handled is an important aspect of the process of making a formal decision about whether plagiarism occurred and what its consequences are. Ideally part of the agreement should be clarity about how to interpret grayscale situations.

2.3.1 SECOND-LANGUAGE STUDENTS

One of the areas where grayscale problems are evident come from non-native speakers trying to write in English (or any other language with which they are only moderately familiar). Younghwa Lee writes in the article "Understanding anti plagiarism software adoption: An extended protection motivation theory perspective":

"Through a variety of naturalistic means of investigation, above all through interviews and examination of novice texts, researchers have achieved increasing understanding of the complexities of novices' intertextual practices which would orthodoxically be labeled as plagiarism, in light of institutional anti-plagiarism policies. ... Previous research with Chinese doctoral science students indicates that for EAL novices who have hardly had any prior experience in academic writing in English, language reuse is an important composing strategy." Lee [2011]

Cultural issues play a role here. This form of "language reuse" may be particularly common among Asian students, since the east Asian languages are sufficiently different that students may have trouble distinguishing between common phrases that many authors might reasonably use, and more precise formulations that trigger plagiarism alerts.

It may not be chance that Asian students, who traditionally must do more rote learning of texts, also have a higher recall for specific phrases. There is a substantial psychological literature about learning and long-term memory.

Bors and MacLeod [1996] write in a chapter on "Individual Differences in Memory":

"Individual differences in WM [Working Memory] capacity have been discovered to correlate with various measures of aptitude and achievement." [p. 421]

"Taken together, this work can be interpreted as evidence that the high-knowledge individuals more consistently tied events to the goal structure and kept the important information in working memory, strategies that are important during both acquisition and remembering. Other research dovetails nicely with this interpretation. … Clearly, knowledge—both general and specific—makes learning and remembering easier, and therefore individuals with higher knowledge have a significant edge." [pp. 426–427]

One can interpret this to mean that scholars with expertise in a particular area may have higher recall for content in that area because they have working memory strategies that let them internalize it. This is not an excuse for deliberate copying, but it can serve as an explanation for modest amounts of apparent copying when other evidence of deliberate plagiarism (such as large blocks of exact text) is lacking.

2.3.2   SELF-PLAGIARISM

As Davis et al. [2012] write in their chapter "Professionalism, Ethics, and Legal Issues":

"Also, to publish all or part of a work of your own in two different publications is considered self-plagiarism and is certainly unethical even if you are the owner of the copyright." [p. 126]

The authors go on to recognize that:

"Plagiarism can also result from simple ignorance in how to reference other works or in sloppy, careless documentation." [p. 126]

Discovering when potential plagiarism is in fact mere sloppiness, or is the result of good memory, or has other anodyne causes is harder than labeling all unreferenced copying as plagiarism per se. Duplicate submissions could also be classified as a form of self-plagiarism.

2.4   PREVENTION

Discussions about how to prevent plagiarism are widespread. A simple search in Google Scholar on "plagiarism prevention" since the year 2000 gets about 1,200 hits and in Science Direct only 42.[3] In general there are two approaches to prevention, one involving education and the other involving detection.

2.4.1   EDUCATION

The educational approach makes the assumption that people do not intend to plagiarise, but do so inadvertently for some of the reasons mentioned above. Gunnarsson et al. [2014] describe an educational approach in their article on "Teaching international students how to avoid plagiarism: Librarians and faculty in collaboration":

---

[3]As of 26 September 2016.

"From the inception of the course, how to properly use citations and referencing in a research paper has been a central issue discussed in the course. Since the majority of the Master students in the course are young people from various countries, plagiarism education has to be related to their diversity of cultures and habits. By learning how to use sources correctly, the students will avoid being suspected of plagiarism. Therefore the focus in this part of the course has not been how to avoid plagiarism, but on learning how to use information sources correctly." [pp. 413–414]

Teaching students how to use sources correctly and how to do citations is a valuable start, but anyone who teaches knows how limited the retention is, if newly learned material is not rehearsed and practiced regularly. A single course outside the context of normal studies may have no more than a passing effect. Certainly it is better than nothing, but it is also no guarantee that students who have had such a course will not commit inadvertent plagiarism, especially if they are in a situation not specifically described in the course.

2.4.2 DETECTION AS PREVENTION

Detection tools are the topic of the next section, but detection as a form of prevention is a separate issue. The argument of David Ploth above that plagiarism is a "fool's game" reflects the hope that plagiarism tools are so reliable that they will reliably and inevitably catch violations. The fact is that not all publishers use plagiarism-detection tools systematically or correctly, and not all editors and reviewers take the time to understand the analysis, so that errors occur both in making false accusations and ignoring problems.

One of the expectations is that detection will result in swift and appropriate punishment. The existence of serial plagiarizers who continue year after year to produce papers that journals must retract or editors must catch is evidence that the deterrence is imperfect. One reason may be the time-lag between being caught and facing consequences. The consequences may also lead to court cases where a person outside of the academy makes a decision, sometimes on the basis of process errors that have nothing to do with the plagiarism itself.

Plagiarism is only one aspect of research integrity, and tools for detecting other aspects are more difficult to design and less widely used. There are some tools now for image manipulation detection, but a person familiar with the technology can easily circumvent them. Image manipulation is just a special case of data falsification, and with data falsification there are no simple equivalents to the copy-detection tools that now assist in plagiarism detection. Nonetheless the idea of detection as a deterrence is common, especially for plagiarism, where the tools are more developed. Lee [2011] writes in his article "Understanding anti-plagiarism software adoption: An extended protection motivation theory perspective":

"Of these countermeasures, systematic detection using anti-plagiarism software provides a pertinent and effective method [33]." [p. 361]

The footnote reference "33" leads to this article, whose title is further evidence of the attitude.

"[33] C. Jocoy, D. DiBiase, Plagiarism by adult learners online: A case study in detection and remediation, *International Review of Research in Open and Distance Learning,* 7(1), (2006) pp. 1–21."

Genuinely reliable detection might well have the desired discouraging effect, but the broad areas of grayscale unclarity work as a countermeasure, and detection is unlikely to have any deterrence effect on those whose putative plagiarism is unintentional. The problem is not so easily solved.

2.5   DETECTION TOOLS

2.5.1   PLAGIARISM TOOLS

There are too many detection tools, especially for plagiarism, to discuss each thoroughly. Debbie Weber-Wulff has systematically tested many plagiarism systems over the years, and has found none that are entirely reliable. Her most recent test was in 2013. She published the results on her institutional server under the title "Plagiarism detection software test 2013" with co-authors Christopher Möer, Jannis Touras, and Elin Zincke:

"Although the results of past years have always demonstrated that such software is not a solution to the problem of plagiarism, most particularly because of constant problems with false positives and false negatives, as well as massive usability problems, many universities still want to purchase such software." [Weber-Wulff et al., 2015, p. 2]

They tested 15 systems, including Turnitin (which they say uses the same database as iThenticate[4]). They appear to measure plagiarism in the percent of words copied and they set up a six-point scale for rating the systems. They concluded:

"There are three systems in the 'partially useful' category, Urkund, Turnitin, and Copyscape. … Because of this extremely mixed result, it is not possible to recommend the use of a particular system, most particularly as there are many different use cases for the various systems and some are particularly useful for specific purposes, but not generally." [p. 14]

They note problems with false positives because of common phrases where plagiarism is not found, as well as problems with false negatives, that is, places where they felt that plagiarism had not been discovered.

To understand what they counted as undiscovered plagiarism, it is important to consider their categorization. The types include: (1) "copy-and-paste," which they say is "the only kind of

---

[4]Colleagues with close ties to the company tell me privately that this is no longer true.

plagiarism that is quickly recognizable and universally agreed on to be plagiarism"; (2) "disguised plagiarism" (including paraphrasing); (3) translation; (4) "shake & paste [where] paragraphs are taken from a number of different sources and compiled, often without a sensible order"; (5) "structural plagiarism[:] Taking the idea of someone else, their chain of arguments, their selection of quotations from other people, or even the footnotes that they use in the same order without giving credit …"; and (6) "pawn sacrifice … in which the plagiarist does give a reference or even a proper quotation, but does not note that the text continues on far beyond the citation, or in which the plagiarist uses the exact wording of the source without any indication that this is, indeed, a word-for-word quotation" [Weber-Wulff et al., 2015, pp. 6–7].

Not everyone would agree that all of these categories are clear instances of plagiarism. The latter two especially could be controversial. A pawn sacrifice could also be considered mere poor practice with no clear attempt to deceive. The idea of structural plagiarism could also include instances where the chain of arguments and references are so standard in a field that many people could come up with similar results. Shake and paste could well be plagiarism, depending on the context and the number of contiguous words involved. None of these categories, including paraphrasing and translation, allow for judgments about differences in the scholarly context. They set an absolute standard that includes every possible circumstance where deliberate copying could occur, without allowance for whether that standard makes sense within the disciplinary or academic context of the time and place.

2.5.2   ITHENTICATE

iThenticate is the best known product for plagiarism discovery among publishers. The service is a product from the same company that provides Turnitin, a service to detect copying in student papers. The company changed its database in 2014 to use Crossref and has rebranded its service to be called "Crossref Similarity Check Powered by iThenticate" (iThenticate, 2016). The move to use Crossref has given iThenticate a more consistent and complete database than it could have had on its own, without changing its interface or (apparently) its algorithms. iThenticate is cautious about its terminology and talks only about a "match overview" rather than using the word "plagiarism." Legal reasons likely play a role. VroniPlag is equally cautious, and uses the phrase "Fremdtextübernahmen" (literally, taking text from elsewhere).

2.5.3   CROWDSOURCING

VroniPlag[5] is an example of the use of crowdsourcing to discover plagiarism, and it is an interesting question to what role crowdsourcing could play in reducing research integrity problems in articles that were exposed via pre-publication servers. It may be that plagiarism rates are lower, but as yet there is no evidence. Even more interesting would be an investigation of whether exposure caught other forms of integrity violations, especially data falsification and image manipulation.

---

[5]See Section 3.2 for more detail about VroniPlag.

2.5.4 IMAGE-MANIPULATION TOOLS

Tools for detecting other forms of research integrity problems are much rarer. A few tools exist to discover certain kinds of image manipulation. Newman [2013] wrote about a number of new tools in his article "The art of detecting data and image manipulation," including Forensic Droplets and Photoshop Actions. The former is free and can be download from the U.S. Office of Research Integrity. He explains that Droplets can be used to:

- "Find out whether an image's light or dark areas have been adjusted.

- Evaluate whether two images may have been obtained from a single source.

- Compare two images."

More about tools to detect image manipulation will be discussed in a later chapter.

Newman [2013] also writes about ways to detect fraudulent data, most of which rely on probability expectations, such as the approach used by "James Mosimann, a bio-statistician at ORI in the 1990s …" ScienceDirect shows over 2,000 hits since the year 2000 for a search on "data NEAR fraud NEAR detection"[6] since the Diederik Stapel case came to light in 2011, but many of these are about financial fraud. Very few studies look specifically at research data fraud. One study that appeared in close conjunction with the Stapel case was by Martin Enserink [2012], who writes:

> "…what fascinates them [psychologists] most is how the new case, which led to the resignation of psychologist Dirk Smeesters of Erasmus University Rotterdam and the requested retraction of two of his papers by his school, came to light: through an unpublished statistical method to detect data fraud. … The technique was developed by Uri Simonsohn, a social psychologist at the Wharton School of the University of Pennsylvania …"

Simonsohn [2013] writes in the article "Just Post It: The Lesson From Two Cases of Fabricated Data Detected by Statistics Alone":

> "To undetectably fabricate data is difficult. It requires both (a) a good understanding of the phenomenon being studied (e.g., what measures of a construct tend to look like, which variables they correlate with and by how much) and (b) a good understanding of how sampling error is expected to influence the data (e.g., how much variation and the kind of variation the estimates of interest should exhibit given the observed sample size and design). In this article, I show that although means and standard deviations can be analyzed in light of these two criteria to identify likely cases of fraud, the availability of raw data makes the task of detection easier and more diagnostic, and hence that of fabrication more difficult and intimidating." [p. 1]

---

[6]As of September 26 2016.

This analysis is interesting also in making clear how much specific subject knowledge is necessary to detect data fraud. It is not like plagiarism, where simple comparisons can detect the problem. A novice in the field would be challenged to say why certain kinds of data are implausible. Simonsohn [2013] writes in the abstract of his article: "I argue that requiring authors to post the raw data supporting their published results has the benefit, among many others, of making fraud much less likely to go undetected." This is another instance of crowd-sourced fraud detection.

2.6   REPLICATION

Replication could be a tool for discovering research integrity problems, under circumstances where there is a reasonable expectation that replication is possible. In the natural sciences there is a long-standing expectation that two scientists should be able to get the same results when following the same procedures on the same materials under the same circumstances. If replication fails, faked data is certainly one of many possible reasons. The social sciences increasingly take replication seriously too, though the variability of context and conditions make reliability harder. Colin Camerer et al. write in an article, "Evaluating replicability of laboratory experiments in economics":

"Replication is now more important than ever, as the reproducibility of results has been questioned in many sciences, such as medicine (2-5), neuroscience (6) and genetics (7, 8)." [Camerer et al., 2016]
Nonetheless:

> "The recent Reproducibility Project Psychology (RPP) replicated 100 original studies published in three top journals in psychology. The vast majority (97) of the original studies reported 'positive findings,' but in the replications the RPP only found a significant effect in the same direction for 36% of these studies (19)." [Camerer et al., 2016]

Although results for the Psychology study are poor, interpreting these results is difficult because many researchers either failed to document the exact conditions of the first test or because those reproducing the experiment were unable to recreate the conditions exactly. Camerer et al. [2016] recommend "that as scientists we should design and document our methods to anticipate replication and make it easy to do." If this happened, and if the rate of successful reproducibility increased, systematic reproduction could become a way to expose data fraud. That does not, however, appear to be the current situation.

CHAPTER 3

Quantifying Plagiarism

3.1 OVERVIEW

This chapter will use the word *matching* to refer to situations where plagiarism checkers have found similar phrases in two or more texts, instead of words like *copying*, which implies intentionality, or *plagiarism*, which implies guilt.

3.1.1 HISTORY

Plagiarism is one of the most commonly discussed and likely one of the most prevalent forms of research integrity violation. In the paper-based world plagiarism was difficult to discover, unless the reader had an excellent memory for text and unless the case was relatively obvious. There was no systematic means of comparing texts quickly and efficiently. At one time simple, blatant plagiarism seemed primarily to occur among undergraduate students, who copied passages from textbooks or from assigned reading. These sources were readily at hand and relevant to the content of the course. Copying from outside literature would have meant extra work, and work avoidance could reasonably be considered a primary reason for students to risk plagiarism—assuming they understood the risk. This kind of copying had the advantage that it made detection easier for instructors with a thorough knowledge of the literature they assigned. Copying from other students was an option too, particularly on exams, and it made detection comparatively easy as long as the numbers remained fairly small.

It has become a commonplace that digital content and internet access have made plagiarism easier to commit as well as to detect. While that is doubtless true, it is only part of the story and part of the history. Librarians have long worked on guides and indexes to facilitate the discovery of academic content, and finding a relevant source for copying content is a first step in any halfway earnest attempt to commit plagiarism. Finding a source did not eliminate the need for copying it by hand onto a paper in the pre-digital, pre-internet world, but entering text by hand costs less time than thinking through how to say the same thing in one's own words. Better discovery tools for appropriate content also made detection more difficult, depending on the size of the library collection, because the range of potential sources became greater than most people could know well enough to recognize quickly. Claims that plagiarism occurred less frequently in a purely paper environment could be true, on the theory that it required more effort, but the apparent reliability and plausibility of such a claim may also be an artifact of a lack of detection. As more and more older content becomes accessible digitally, it could be interesting to see how much matching modern tools can find.

3.1.2   DEFINITION

Plagiarism is hard to define in any precise way. At the simplest level it is copying texts from other authors and using them as if they were their own. This definition does little, however, to define where content overlap goes beyond an acceptable level and turns into an integrity violation. In practice the academic world leaves these decisions to the professor or publisher or editor, but that makes decisions about where the boundaries lie arbitrary and inconsistent, because there is no evidence that two persons will necessarily come to the same conclusion, except in some extreme and obvious cases. This can lead to a kind of vigilantism where self-appointed plagiarism-hunters set their own rules and make damaging accusations. One of the key goals of this chapter is to suggest an approach that looks for metrics that can establish those boundaries and thus to make the definition more precise.

A more precise definition of plagiarism requires both context and metrics. Context is important because the different disciplines tolerate standard phrases differently and value the uniqueness of expression differently. Metrics matter so that those judging have more than a gut feeling whether the matching has overreached the limit of what is acceptable. Metrics for plagiarism need to take the number of words, phrases, paragraphs, and pages into account. Simple counts do not suffice. They need to be seen not only in an appropriate disciplinary context, but also in a historical context, since standards change over time. Such numbers generally do not exist at present, and a part of the process of making a more precise definition is to discover what those numbers should represent and how to get them.

3.1.3   PAGES AND PERCENTS

The most common metrics available today have to do with the overall number of pages where matching has occurred, and the percentage of the text suspected of being copied. Systems like iThenticate make it possible to exclude certain areas, like bibliographies, and let the user set a threshold for sending warning messages about plagiarism—the system is sophisticated enough not to assume that all matches are a problem.

VroniPlag in Germany provides a color coding that shows which pages have more than 75% matching (red), 50% matching (maroon), or some matches (black). Pages with no matches are in white. As a visual device, this is very convincing and effective. Both iThenticate and VroniPlag (and other plagiarism detection projects) provide page-level detail about which passages they suspect, and the details in both iThenticate and VroniPlag are reliable. They indicate an overall judgment in the form of total percentage or via the mass of color. When most of a work is colored red (over 75% matching) in VroniPlag, or the percentage is high, the evidence looks conclusive and it may well be, especially in cases where whole paragraphs were matched word-for-word, but paragraphs with matching from multiple sources may also tell a different story on closer analysis.

Absolutely clear-cut situations are rare. A single matched mass—whole sentences and paragraphs from the same source—certainly counts as a strong indication of plagiarism, without some other explanation. More often the matching is less contiguous words or phrases rather than paragraphs. There is no standard measure today for how contiguous the matching must be to count as a problem, and the measure may well depend on social practice and expectations within specific disciplines. Contiguity can be measured in several ways.

Simple counting.

This count measures how many contiguous words match contiguous words from another source. In the following example, "m" plus a number represents words matching a text elsewhere, m1 for example, and "w" plus a number represents any other non-matching word. The five-word sentence "m1 m2 w1 m3 m4" contains two sets of two contiguous words, which could be counted as a single 4 / 5 or 80% overlap, or it could be counted as two instances of 2 / 5 or 40% matching, which may be preferred if the words come from different sources.

An issue here is whether the instances are additive. The following example could possibly be more serious because of the longer string of contiguous words: m1 m2 m3 m4 w1. This could still be counted as 4 / 5 or 80%, but the potential for plagiarism seems greater because the string is longer. A lot depends on the nature of the words, both in terms of content and in terms of discipline. Discipline-specific issues will be examined later.

Intensified counting.

Function words are words that carry minimal meaning in and of themselves, but play a role in the grammar and structure of a sentence. The following sentence has three function words (*the, to, the*) and three non-function words (man, walked, store): "The man walked to the store." Different function words may change the meaning subtly, but the substance of what happens remains largely unchanged; for example: "A man walked into a store." If the three non-function words all match some other source, but the three function words do not, the matching ratio might be 2 / 5 (*man walked*) and 1 / 5 (*store*), or totaled 3 / 5 (60%). If the function words are not counted, since they are easily changed in order to obscure matching algorithms, then the same sentence has a 3 / 3 or 100% match.

Stripping out function words can help to determine whether plagiarism occurred, even if the plagiarist obscured the fact, but it must be used with caution. An overlap of less than 100% of the meaningful words can also lead to false conclusions. In the following sentence, for example, there is 66% (2 / 3) matching, but the change of the subject (cat instead of man) makes it seem more like a coincidence: The cat walked to the store.

3.1.4 CONTEXT, QUOTES, AND REFERENCES

Context matters in almost all plagiarism cases. Using quotation marks and specific references is always the safest approach, but this standard needs to be applied with care. The point of finding plagiarism is to uphold the rigor and reliability of scholarship, not to hold authors to an arbitrary set of rules. When rules are applied, it is important that the rules be clear and justifiable, ideally by empirical data based on the actual community practice. Often it is hard to describe research results without using some words others have used for the same topic. Matching in a statistical results section may reflect a standardized vocabulary for the kind of test or the discipline. Matches may also reflect a good memory for text, a standard phrase, or an overuse of phrases that seem standard in an attempt to state technical matters correctly. Here the metrics require comparison with other texts from the same discipline and the same type of content to determine reliably whether the overlap in vocabulary is greater than usual.

Time is a factor in judging older works. The use of quotation marks (or italics or sometimes indentation) for any text from another author is largely taken for granted today, but the expectations have varied over time. It is easy to find articles in which established authors, past and present, have paraphrased what others have said. This is especially common in literature review sections, where the author has the obligation to report the content of relevant works, and may not want to fill the text with quoted passages. How closely the wording of a paraphrased section must be to the original text before requiring quotation marks around multiple exact phrases is unclear and open to debate. Empirical data about the practice are needed.

The location of references can be an issue. References are normally near the content being cited—either at the end of a quote or a sentence or occasionally a paragraph. While a missing reference is certainly a problem, a more distant reference is not automatically an attempt to deceive, since the reference was at least there. Location can be a style issue for some authors. The intent may also have been to encompass the whole content of the paragraph or other unit. This is where some form of grayscale evaluation helps. In modern times distant references are less widely accepted than in the past, but circumstances vary. Data from comparable works under comparable circumstances are needed to measure this reliably.

General knowledge may require no quotation marks and no reference. Sometimes well-known experts in a field will relate information without references because the information has become an integral part of their personal knowledge base. The fact that different people relate the same facts using similar formulations may not be a sign of copying, but of the degree to which the information has become generally known. This is hard to measure, and varies greatly from discipline to discipline. The issue will be discussed further in the sections on the humanities, social sciences, and natural sciences.

3.1.5   SENTENCES, PARAGRAPHS, AND OTHER UNITS

When measuring the number of matches in a work, a defined unit helps to provide an appropriate relative size and context for the number. Metrics using just the percentage of matches are not necessarily proof of plagiarism, as will be discussed below, but such metrics are flags to show how likely it is to represent a genuine research integrity problem.

Three suspect words out of ten is far more troubling than three out of a thousand. Sentences or paragraphs or pages as the measurement units are natural units within the work, but they have the weaknesses that the lengths may vary greatly within the work and in comparison to other works. Matches in two whole sentences in a paragraph can be seen as an indication of plagiarism, but two very short sentences in a long paragraph imply a different signal than two very long sentences in a short paragraph.

The percent of matches per page is a relatively common indicator in plagiarism detection, but even the amount of content on a standardized A4 page varies because of spacing and font sizes. In theory the metrics could be standardized by copying all the content into standardized pages with the same spacing, fonts, and length, but other context information could be lost. A unit such as a set number of words could also be an option, but calculating the number of matches in, for example, three hundred word chunks could split the matched text across two chunks, so that each instance appears to be smaller. The fact is that there are no perfect units.

In the end the units that make the most sense are the ones that the authors used. A whole paragraph with high-congruency matches (that is, a large number of sequential words from a single source) could indicate that the authors took the content knowingly from another source and dropped it essentially unchanged into their own text. High-congruency matching generally signals an easy decision and the unit size may not matter. Situations where other words or phrases interrupt the text matches are more challenging and it helps to have a base of comparison using units that make sense within the context of the work. A measure such as "30%" potential matches only makes sense in the end if the base unit for the percentage is clear.

3.1.6   SELF-PLAGIARISM

Self-plagiarism is a topic that cuts across disciplines. It may be marginally more common in the natural sciences, where originality of expression is less valued, but can occur anywhere in scholarship. There is no consensus about self-plagiarism. Many people feel that authors should formally quote and cite themselves whenever they take content from a work they published previously, but this can also lead to accusations that the author is trying to increase their citation count. Some citation systems count self-citation, others make an effort not to.

The metrics of self-plagiarism are not fundamentally different than those of other forms of copying. In general the larger the blocks of consecutive words in reused text, the more problematic. Taking whole paragraphs from one's previously published work without any attribution is different than taking a few sentences or phrases, and is not entirely fair to a publisher, who may expect some greater degree of originality. Most publishers would regard an article that is 50% self-plagiarized as unacceptably unoriginal. An article with 10% self-plagiarism may well be tolerable, especially if the author acknowledges the previous source, even without using quotation marks. The only rule is a vague rule of thumb.

The way in which the amount of self-plagiarism can be calculated is no different than for other forms of matching, but it is worth separating instances of self-plagiarism from other matches to give reviewers the option of judging it on its own. Even if it is considered unacceptable, it is not stealing from someone else. This is particularly true of duplicate publications, which steal only space in a journal.

3.2   IN THE HUMANITIES

3.2.1   OVERVIEW

Plagiarism is an issue of significance in the humanities, because there, more than in the social or natural sciences, language and the choice of words determine the persuasiveness and the quality of the analysis of a scholarly work. Words in the humanities represent both the data and the analysis. This means that the sensitivity about matches is greater, regardless of whether the matching congruency is high or low.

By some measures the number of public instances of plagiarism in the humanities is relatively few. Retraction Watch lists one in film studies, three in history, six in literature, and one in poetry for a total of ten in fields that clearly belong to the humanities.[1] The small size of this number has several possible reasons. One is that Retraction Watch has a strong natural science focus, and simply does not list all cases. Another reason could be that the publishers of monographs, the publication form of preference for many humanists, do less plagiarism checking. It is also possible, maybe even likely, that humanists plagiarize less because they care more about their own choice of words, or that they are better at disguising plagiarism by rewriting texts.

When plagiarism in the humanities occurs, it sometimes gets a lot of public notice. In the online journal Slate, for example, Plotz [2002] wrote the article "The Plagiarist: Why Stephen Ambrose is a Vampire." His article accuses Stephen Ambrose of repeated plagiarism without giving any metrics other than to refer to "lifted sentences" and "swiped phrases and passages." He claims that the number of works containing plagiarism is significant and that "[t]he list of writers snared over the years is long and depressingly impressive." The six names that follow are well known, including "Martin Luther King Jr., who lifted much of his dissertation." The case of Martin Luther King is well known.

In October 1991 the *New York Times* reported that: "A committee of scholars appointed by Boston University concluded today that the Rev. Martin Luther King Jr. plagiarized passages in his dissertation for a doctoral degree at the university 36 years ago." No metrics are given in the article. According to the "King's Dissertation" website: "The King Papers Project in 1991 estimated that 52% of Chapter 2 of the thesis was plagiarized—transcribed from the work of other authors without any indication that the section was an exact reproduction." This number is not on the King Papers project website at Stanford and cannot easily be confirmed. Most sources seem to agree that some plagiarism occurred in the chapter on Paul Tillich, where King was explaining Tillich's ideas. Quotation marks were missing and explicit references were missing.

Copying certainly occurred, but King's reputation and his life made the university unwilling to retract his degree. The consequences of humanities plagiarism are highly various. Most people do not have a reputation like King's to protect them, but because of his reputation, no one asked whether the copying vitiated the academic value of the work, or represented no more than a serious formal mistake in an otherwise acceptable work. This passive reaction occurred in spite of

---

[1] As of 26 September 2016.

the fact many humanists regard any plagiarism as overstepping the limit of what is acceptable. In practice the answer to plagiarism cases is not always clear-cut.

The use of standard phrases can under some circumstances create misleading hits in match-detection systems. A search in the Google Ngram viewer can find many exact phrases that authors repeat over and over again. One example is the phrase "the author of this work," which uses the maximum five-word string for searching in the Ngram viewer. Since the Ngram viewer gives its results in percentages, it helps to understand the actual number of hits by using the "English one million" corpus, since it offers a fixed size. The result is that the phrase is in constant use since at least 1800 with a high point in 1816, then a long decline followed by a steady increase since the 1980s up to 2007 (which appears to be the most recent data). Most reviewers would not see such a phrase as having enough meaning to be copied, but systems that check for matches can and often do pick up such phrases.

3.2.2 PARAGRAPH-LENGTH EXAMPLES

This section will examine a number of humanities texts where plagiarism has been suspected. In some cases the names of the authors will not be used, since they are actual ongoing cases, even if the texts themselves are public. The texts themselves are important here only as examples. Artificial examples would do, but would not have quite the same verisimilitude.

Princeton

The first example text comes from the "Academic Integrity" web page at Princeton University [2016], where the university provides three examples of plagiarism in humanities texts. The first example comes from text that plagiarized a passage in "Alvin Kernan, The Playwright as Magician. New Haven: Yale University Press, 1979. pp. 102–103." The "verbatim plagiarism" of this text includes three segments of contiguous words. The first has seven words, the second has 24 words, and the third has 73 words. A single word that does not come from the original text ("he") separates the three segments. Twenty-one other words at the beginning of the paragraph also did not come from Kernan. This means that 82% of the paragraph was copied. The website treats this as a clear case of plagiarism, and with no other context information, the evidence of plagiarism seems convincing.

The second example is also copying from Kernan. In this example there are six segments of contiguous words, one of three words, one of eight words, one of six words, one of thirteen words, one of five words, and one of ten words out of a paragraph of 104 words. There are non-copied segments of three, eleven, eleven, eight, and two words between the copied text. The overall percentage of copied text is 43%. Some of the phrases could be considered relatively standard, "pretense of madness," for example, finds a number of matches in the Google Ngram viewer. The coincidence of so many contiguous words in a single paragraph is, however, convincing. The website comments that

"In the case above, if the writer had rewritten the entire paragraph and used only Alvin Kernan's phrase 'high heroic terms' without properly quoting and acknowledging its source, the writer would have plagiarized." [Princeton University, 2016]

The Google Ngram viewer finds no hits for the phrase "high heroic terms," but a cautious plagiarism judge ought perhaps not exclude the possibility that two writers invented the same short phrase independently when discussing the same literary work without further evidence.

The third example has no overlap in contiguous words. Because the plagiarism argument is more complicated, the two paragraphs are copied in their entirety below:

Original source (text)
"From time to time this submerged or latent theater in Hamlet becomes almost overt. It is close to the surface in Hamlet's pretense of madness, the "antic disposition" he puts on to protect himself and prevent his antagonists from plucking out the heart of his mystery. It is even closer to the surface when Hamlet enters his mother's room and holds up, side by side, the pictures of the two kings, Old Hamlet and Claudius, and proceeds to describe for her the true nature of the choice she has made, presenting truth by means of a show. Similarly, when he leaps into the open grave at Ophelia's funeral, ranting in high heroic terms, he is acting out for Laertes, and perhaps for himself as well, the folly of excessive, melodramatic expressions of grief."

Paraphrasing the text while maintaining the basic paragraph and sentence structure
"Almost all of Shakespeare's Hamlet can be understood as a play about acting and the theater. For example, in Act 1, Hamlet pretends to be insane in order to make sure his enemies do not discover his mission to revenge his father's murder. The theme is even more obvious when Hamlet compares the pictures of his mother's two husbands to show her what a bad choice she has made, using their images to reveal the truth. Also, when he jumps into Ophelia's grave, hurling his challenge to Laertes, Hamlet demonstrates the foolishness of exaggerated expressions of emotion."

The website comments:

"Almost nothing of Kernan's original language remains in this rewritten paragraph. However, the key idea, the choice and order of the examples, and even the basic structure of the original sentences are all taken from the source. This is another clear example of plagiarism." [Princeton University, 2016]

Many plagiarism-checking systems would not flag this paragraph as plagiarized because the overlapping words are mainly names or facts: Hamlet, Ophelia, Laertes, theater, and grave. Both paragraphs have four sentences and the sequencing is similar. The words "theater" and "Hamlet" appear in both first sentences. "Ophelia," "grave," and "Laertes" appear in the fourth (last) sentence. The topics of the middle two sentences have no words in common, but again several facts: Hamlet pretending to be insane and Hamlet using the two pictures. The putative plagiarism here consists of ideas, not expression, and the author of the second paragraph could reasonably argue that the similarity is an accident of the structure and contents of the play itself. Here is where the humanities diverge from the sciences. The description of a sequence of operations in a chemical experiment is in effect a mechanical recitation of facts, regardless of the words used, but in the humanities the description of a sequence of human actions in a play takes on a more personal character because the word choice and the sequence is not considered mechanical.

Measuring plagiarism in an example like this is theoretically possible with systems sufficiently intelligent to discern the overlap of meaning in the two paragraphs, assuming that an overlap in meaning without an overlap of words counts as plagiarism. The author of the Princeton website has no doubt, but it is a less clear-cut example than the first case with 82% overlap in words. The plagiarism determination here may depend on whether the reader understands the sentences as interpretation, or as an essentially factual summary of the situation. The first paragraph is rich in interpretative description, while the second focuses more on the facts of the story. Even if most humanists agreed that the second paragraph plagiarized ideas from the first, a panel of non-humanists might have doubts, especially if this were a lone problematic example in a longer work. As always, context matters.

Indiana

Another example of humanities plagiarism comes from a PDF flyer called "Examples of Plagiarism, and of Appropriate Use of Others' Words and Ideas" at Indiana University [2011]. This example uses the following passage from "Lizzie Borden: A Case Book of Family and Crime in the 1890s by Joyce Williams et al. (p. 1)":

> "The rise of industry, the growth of cities, and the expansion of the population were the three great developments of late nineteenth century American history. As new, larger, steam-powered factories became a feature of the American landscape in the East, they transformed farm hands into industrial laborers, and provided jobs for a rising tide of immigrants. With industry came urbanization—the growth of large cities (like Fall River, Massachusetts, where the Bordens lived) which became the centers of production as well as of commerce and trade."

The first plagiarism example is relatively standard with nine instances of overlapping contiguous words: 7+5+3+3+4+4+2+4+7 = 39 words overlapping out of 78 total or 50% overlap. The final set of seven words actually contained some rearrangement of the words with no change of meaning. Some phrases are very standard. The phrase "the growth of cities," for example, had a high point in the Google Ngram viewer in 1921. The phrase "and provided jobs for" is also far from unique. Nonetheless the coincidence of these common phrases strengthens the impression that the metric gives.

The next example has only eleven contiguous words in common with the original, and only one phrase "Fall River, where the Borden family lived" that with the omission of one word overlaps with the original:

"Fall River, where the Borden family lived, was typical of northeastern industrial cities of the nineteenth century. Steam-powered production had shifted labor from agriculture to manufacturing, and as immigrants arrived in the US, they found work in these new factories. As a result, populations grew, and large urban areas arose. Fall River was one of these manufacturing and commercial centers (Williams 1)."

The percentage of overlap is 12%. The flyer calls this example:

"... acceptable paraphrasing because the writer:

- accurately relays the information in the original

- uses her own words

- lets her reader know the source of her information."

The reference at the end is an important factor, but it is not immediately obvious why this passage "more accurately relays the information" than the one with 50% matching. The passage is not fundamentally different in its matching metrics than the third example from Princeton. The content overlap is the same, even though some phrases were rearranged. The chief factor that makes it different from the Princeton case is the reference at the end. That matters, of course, even though there can be some disagreement about the placement of a reference, when there is no direct quote.

3.2.3   BOOK-LENGTH EXAMPLES

Book-length examples are more important in the humanities than in other areas, because so much of the humanities scholarship appears in book formats, but the scale of books present problems for establishing plagiarism metrics because of the variety of possible units for comparison. Not all parts of books are equally important, and irregularities in one part may be less damaging to the ultimate scholarly value than in others, except for those who believe that any plagiarism destroys the whole work.

Because detailed examples of book-length plagiarism are harder to find in English than in German, this section will rely heavily on German-language examples. One reason that German content is more available is that VroniPlag has undertaken systematic plagiarism checking in publicly available dissertations, partly by machine, partly by hand, on a large number of digitally available German dissertations. This activity grew out of the plagiarism scandal of the former defense minister, Karl-Theodor zu Guttenberg.

Much of the original work on GuttenPlag and now VroniPlag involves crowdsourcing, that is, large numbers of essentially anonymous helpers who look for evidence of matches. Only a few names are well known: Roland Schimmel, a professor for economic law at the Frankfurt University of Applied Sciences, Debora Weber-Wulff, a professor for computer science at the Berlin Hochschule für Technik und Wirtschaft, Gerhard Dannemann, a law school professor at Humboldt-Universität zu Berlin, and Denis Basak, a law school professor at the Goethe-Universität in Frankfurt [Klovert, 2015]. These four help to ensure accuracy.

The information on VroniPlag is public, and anyone can read the accusations. Nonetheless plagiarism accusations can destroy reputations and careers. While VroniPlag publishes the names, this monograph will only use the abbreviation that VroniPlag uses as its reference point. Anyone who wants to find the name and the details can find them with the abbreviation. Some examples represent cases under consideration by universities. This monograph deliberately offers no judgment about whether or not these works should be considered plagiarized. The goal is to develop and examine metrics that could be of use to institutional commissions now and in the future when making decisions about whether a work represents a research integrity violation.

The first example is labeled as "Asc" in VroniPlag. Here are the first two paragraphs of the author's own abstract to provide some context:

"Only a few print media focus on allergies as a matter of public interest. For this reason the dissertation analyzes the presentation of allergies in English and American lifestyle magazines.

This thesis examines the propagation of medical knowledge via the media. It shows if and how the media contribute to health education and information about illness, its relevance, diagnostic investigation as well as therapy. The main focus is on those words which are used as metaphors. They represent an important subject of Susan Sontag's essay "Illness as Metaphor" which demonstrates the presentation of illness, the use of stereotypes and thus raises issues about illness being a social and cultural matter of interest." [ASC, 2011, p. ii]

A Page as a Unit of Measure

A page is a common unit of measure in plagiarism metrics. In a typical example, the metric is given as: "Anzahl der Seiten mit Funden" [number of pages with discovered text] [Vroniplag, 2016] and then a percentage that represents the percentage of pages where matches were discovered divided by the page total for the work. While this probably averages out over many examples, it can give a misleadingly high count if relatively few sentences per page have problems, but many pages were affected. And if the concentration of matches was high, but limited to just a few pages, it could give a misleadingly low count. For VroniPlag, the pages are relatively uniform in size, since Germany uses A4 for dissertations.

VroniPlag provides what it calls a "barcode" to show where matches occurred. It is a long rectangle that represents the pages in a work, and the pages are color-coded. Light blue stands for front matter and end matter, such as the bibliography. White represents unaffected pages. Black indicates some matching, maroon represents matching that is more than 50% of the page, and red represents over 75%. This creates a very effective visual based on the pages and their location within the work. It does not provide any indication of major section breaks.

The first place where VroniPlag finds matches in ASC is page eight in chapter two. To give some context information, the chapter heading is "Medizinhistorische und kulturwissenschaftliche Verortung von Allergien" [Historical medical and cultural localization of allergies] and the section is called "Betrachtungsweisen von Allergien" [Ways of looking at allergies]. The color is black, meaning less that 50% of the page was affected. The page has six segments of contiguous words that match another source: 77, 11, 7, 7, 3 and 3 words for a total of 108 words on a page with a total of 291 words or 37%. Interestingly the largest segment contains two footnote references to a web page that is no longer available and that appears to change regularly. At this time it is impossible to say whether it represented a reference to the source of the quotation, but the possibility cannot be excluded. If the portion with the flawed footnote is removed, then the matching is down to 11%.

An important question for those accused of plagiarism is whether flawed footnotes count as an indication of good intent, or whether the contents should be included in the total number of matches because no quotation marks or other indication of intentional copying was used. Quotation marks or italics or other indications of intentional copying are certainly part of good practice, but even in their absence the presence of a footnote could reasonably play a role in the judgment, except where there is reason to think that the footnote itself was deliberately faked.

On another randomly chosen page in the same work, p. 58, there are three footnotes. The first includes five segments of contiguous words and the footnote refers exactly to the page that the VroniPlag searchers found. The second footnote appears to refer to eight segments and to a different (older) source than VroniPlag found. The third footnote also refers to a different and apparently older source. The remaining four copied segments on this page have no footnote, but early on the following page there is a reference to the same source where VroniPlag found source text. Using pages as the unit potentially masks what may be a consistent pattern of using references. If all of the segments matched in VroniPlag count, then the segments add up to 244 out of 327 words, or 75% of the page. If the footnotes put the text into a (lesser) poor-practice category, the contents would remain problematic, but would not count as plagiarism per se, so the percentage would be zero.

The Section as a Unit of Measure

The section with the most red in VroniPlag is one called "Metaphorisierung der Krankheit" [Turning Sickness into a Metaphor] on pages 55–90. This includes 27 of the 40 pages where VroniPlag found matching (67.5%). The breakdown is as follows:

pages 55–61 are red, meaning over 75% matching.

pages 62–63 are black, meaning less than 50% matching

pages 65–66 are black,

pages 69–71 are black,

page 72 is red,

page 73 is black,

pages 75–76 are red,

pages 77–78 are black,

page 79 is red,

pages 80–81 are black,

page 82 is maroon, meaning 50–75% matching,

pages 85–86 are red,

page 87 is black

The other pages are white, which means they are unaffected. This adds up to 13 pages with matching over 75%, 13 pages with matching under 50%, and one page with matching between 50 and 75%.

This means that instead of 27 pages with matching out of 40 in this section, a more accurate count would be between 20.25 pages (calculating each red page as 100% copied, each maroon as 75% copied, and each black page as 50%) or 14.95 pages (calculating each red page as 80% copied, each maroon page as 65%, and each black page as 30%). This means that the percent of matches in the section is roughly between 50% and 37% of the content, rather than 67.5% of the number of pages. The difference is significant.

The pages also contain 43 footnotes, and the footnotes on the following pages point to the same source as VroniPlag on ten pages: 55, 56, 57, 58, 59, 60, 61, 62, 63, 78. VroniPlag found a source not referenced in the text on 17 pages: 65, 66, 69, 70, 71, 72, 73, 75, 76, 77, 79, 80, 81, 82, 85, 86, 87. On one page, 77, the title in the footnote itself is marked as copied, which seems overzealous. In none of these cases did the author use quotation marks to make it clear what text came from the source, and which phrases were the author's own words. Nonetheless in at least 37% of the pages, the author provided an attribution that VroniPlag has, in effect, confirmed. If those pages are not counted, the number of unattributed matches in the section is at most on 17 out of the 40 pages or 42.5%, and since 12 of the 17 pages are black, one is maroon, and only four are red, the maximum amount of matching would then be 10.75 pages out of 40 or 27%. That amount is not trivial, but is different than the initial 67.5% for the section based purely on the page numbers.

The detail is important because plagiarism hunters, including software systems that hunt plagiarism, tend to be aggressive is looking for evidence, and often want to expose people whom they feel have violated an ethical standard of importance to them. In the case of VroniPlag, the missing quotation marks clearly matter as a sign of plagiarism, and in a simple black-and-white judgment, they represent a genuine integrity breach. In a grayscale judgment, however, the presence of a reference could change the situation. Not indicating exactly what the author copied from a source is bad practice, but at least it indicates that the author referred to the original and did not intend to hide where the content came from. A further complication comes from the quality and nature of the references themselves.

A reference to an ever-changing internet page is an extremely poor quality reference, because it is impossible to tell what it said originally, even using the WayBack Machine of the Internet Archive, since the Internet Archive makes only occasional snapshots. Another problem with some references in this section is that they cite older works than the sources that VroniPlag found. It would take significant time and effort to discover whether the VroniPlag sources were actually taking content from the sources the author cited. It could be that the author in fact copied from the later sources and just used that source's source in the footnotes. A grayscale analysis takes significantly more time and effort than a black-and-white one, and the metrics can be very different.

This section in question is part of a literature review, and a literature review presents special problems because its purpose implies that the author is repeating what other authors have said. There are many ways to handle that without risking matching problems, including exact quotes from the sources with commentary on them by the author. Nonetheless it is not unusual, and often reads better, if an author makes some attempt to summarize what others have said without blocks of quotes, but any attempt at summarizing also risks repeating key-words and key formulations from the original. Humanities scholars may be reluctant to treat a literature review section differently from other parts of a work, but in other disciplinary areas, as will be discussed below, the attitude is more flexible.

The Whole Work as a Unit of Measure

VroniPlag claims to have documented plagiarism ("Plagiatsfundstellen") on 40 out of the 168 pages of the work containing content (that is, not front matter or back matter), or 23.8% of all pages [Vroniplag, 2016]. Their wording is careful not to say that 23.8% of the work was plagiarized, only that that percentage of pages contain matching. Pages are relatively easy to count, and when dealing with a book-length work, it offers a certain efficiency and gives a broad overview, but obscures some details. For example, on 14 pages, the author gives a reference to the same work that VroniPlag cites, which means that 26 of the 40 problematic pages have no reference to the same source, which reduces the putative unreferenced matches to 15.5% if one takes a generous attitude toward referencing.

For those for whom any plagiarism is unacceptable, it does not matter whether the amount is 15.5% or 23.8%, but 15.5% comes closer to a number that some editors would treat as discovery system noise and would not investigate further. If the actual number of matches based on the color codes is included, then the percentage falls further. Using the same calculations as above, the number of whole pages with plagiarism is 19.25 and the overall percent is 11.5%.

One of the issues that can matter in judging plagiarism is where it occurs in the book. Matches in the foreword or the literature review may matter less to some scholars than matches in the analysis or conclusions. The reason is that the first two locations are primarily context setting. A reader may expect less originality there, especially in the literature review, because the author may primarily be talking about what others have written. Insofar as people in the humanities have good memories for text, that capability can work against them if they are writing from memory and are reproducing arguments or information from other works.

Many reviewers have a healthy skepticism about claims of semi-photographic memory, and there appears to be no scientific evidence that true photographic memory exists, but there are well known examples of people with specialized knowledge remembering complex combinations with exceptional accuracy. Chess grand masters are a common example. Actors also can learn to recite scripts with ease after going through them several times—a good verbal memory is one of the qualifications for the job. In a situation where an author may have read and reread key works, the possibility that they have so integrated the words and sequence of ideas into their mind that they regard them as their own should not automatically be excluded. The point is not to excuse copying from others, but to distinguish between intentionally taking the ideas and expression of others and doing it inadvertently.

3.3   IN THE SOCIAL SCIENCES

3.3.1   OVERVIEW

In the Anglo-American world, the social sciences represent a separate disciplinary grouping that is neither the humanities nor the natural sciences, but this is not universally true. German universities, for example, traditionally separate disciplines into the Geisteswissenschaften [humanities] or the Naturwissenschaften [natural sciences]. This monograph will use the Anglo-American distinction partly because this is an English-language work, partly because the concept of the social sciences is widely recognized today in publishing, and mainly because the concept helps to distinguish a group of disciplines that share the humanists concern for language and the natural scientists' reliance on data.

Which disciplines belong to the social sciences is far from strict. Sociology and political science are almost always social sciences. Ethnography and history are examples of fields whose classification varies with the institution. Psychology often belongs to the social sciences, but may also be included with the natural sciences or with medicine. There was also a time when universities regarded psychology as part of philosophy. Economics once clearly belonged to the social sciences, but may also belong to a separate school of business. For the purposes of this monograph, a social science may be any discipline that relies heavily on a balance of empirical data and verbal explanation.

The use of statistics is not in itself a hallmark of the social sciences, but it frequently plays a role in the disciplines, and statistics has a language of its own in the form of standard phrases that describe the nature of particular statistical tests, and the type of outcome. The fact that these phrases are highly standardized means that they often appear in systems that look for matches. The formal structure of statistical evaluation can lead to longer passages that use almost the same phrases and vary only a few key words. For example, the phrase "reach a level of significance" gets a large number of hits in the Google Ngram viewer after 1945. Science Direct finds the phrase 24 times in social science articles since the beginning of 2000.[2] This means that a frequency measure for standard phrases is an important metric for cases of potential plagiarism in the social sciences.

The same problem with standard phrases can be true in non-statistical works as well. A check of a random sample of articles in the social science classification of Science Direct in the Google Ngram viewer finds hits over many years for the following phrases: "illustrated in the following equation" (since 1843), "in examining the reasons" (since 1800), "part of a larger study" (since 1900). The social sciences explicitly try to build on past results, as the natural sciences have long done, and in the end there may be a limited number of ways of describing certain outcomes.

3.3.2   EXAMPLE 1

This example is an article that was submitted to a social science-oriented journal. The editor of the journal wanted advice about whether to reject this article for plagiarism, and clearly the article must be presented in an anonymized form. iThenticate gave a match percentage of 48%, which far exceeded the limit set for automatic rejection. Nonetheless some metrics on common phrases were worth considering, because so many appeared in the article. On the first two pages the following phrases that iThenticate marked appear in Science Direct: "are not in conflict with the" (27 times), "based entirely on the assumption that" (two times), "all of these assumptions" (28 times). Phrases not found in Science Direct were: "might behave in theory," "reality aside we would like to," "we executed a trace, over the course of several years"—the sub-phrase "over the course of several years" did, however, appear 56 times. The fact that half the phrases on the first two pages are relatively common does not alter the unusual coincidence that in some cases iThenticate found them in the same two works in essentially the same order.

In this article iThenticate found 68 matches from 43 sources, and it may be significant that for 33 sources, only one match was found. That was a very high distribution of sources and, if the author plagiarized deliberately, the person went to considerable trouble to find passages in different works. Those passages that came from the same source are not generally contiguous, and almost none are full sentences. The six segments from the largest source have fourteen separate phrases and numerous individual words. If the author plagiarized, much of it appears to be unattributed paraphrasing. There are some footnotes in the passages that iThenticate marked, but none appear to lead to the same source that iThenticate found.

The size of the marked phrases and the distance between them is a metric that helps to measure the potential for plagiarism. In a short article like this, it is possible to analyze the number of words between marked phrases and the number of sentences between marked segments. This metric gives the results found in Table 3.1 starting from the beginning.

---

[2]Figures as of September 26, 2016.

Table 3.1: Sentences marked in iThenticate

Number	Marking
2 contiguous sentences	marked as coming in part from two different sources
1 sentence	with no marking
1 sentence	marked as coming in part from one source
1 sentence	with no marking
16 contiguous sentences	marked as coming in part from eleven different sources
3 sentences	with no marking
20 contiguous sentences	marked as coming in part from twelve different sources
5 sentences	with no marking
5 sentences	marked as coming in part from five different sources
1 sentence	with no marking
14 sentences	marked as coming in part from ten different sources

As the entries in this list suggest, a very significant proportion of the article is marked as copied. What is especially interesting and unusual is the overlap of sources. It seems hard to believe that a sentence with four different sources can really be considered as deliberately copied in any normal sense. The small number of contiguous sentences from any single source is also unusual for plagiarism. In some cases iThenticate has marked a single word, for example "the" or "this" at the beginning of a sentence following a sentence marked for matching. While the use of the same word in the following sentence could indicate copying, with simple function words like "that," it could well be pure coincidence.

In this example, there are almost no sentences that iThenticate marked as coming entirely from a single source. The sources are also very heavily internet based: 22 internet sources vs. 21 articles. Some internet sources where iThenticate said that it found matches are unusual in a scholarly article. iThenticate found six matches on the site "http://sci.sexy23.de/2." The self-description on this site is: "Well, this site gets random content from SCIgen—An Automatic CS Paper Generator. Its goal is to investigate the impact of randomly generated content on search engine listings" [Sexy23-anonymous, 2016]. Another unusual source where iThenticate found four matches is "http://www.lovegrp.com/". It is a Korean site that appears to be about the Hanwoori family. iThenticate also included one match from a plainly political website ("http://theseunitedstates.org/") whose avowed purpose has nothing to do with the content of the paper. The set of words that iThenticate found in a 16-word line were: "will many of the faced by today's... we ... that." These are not isolated examples. One of the matches was also the title of the journal. Even a highly reputed tool like iThenticate can give results that need careful examination.

The article itself lists 17 sources in its reference list, all of them to scholarly articles, although some are relatively obscure. Reference 11, for example, appears in the middle of a sentence after the phrase "A recent unpublished undergraduate dissertation." The journal that the author gives is not in WorldCat, though of course a typing error could be possible. iThenticate found the passage in an online journal called "digg.com," which appears to change regularly. A random search for another title in the reference list, "Journal of Secure, empathic Configurations" also finds nothing in WorldCat. The same is true for the "Journal of Semantic Linear-time Algorithms." Missing entries in WorldCat are no guarantee that sources were made up, but this is a metric that must raise suspicions about data falsification.

Overall the record for the article seems bad. Out of 93 sentences, 74 or 81% were flagged as having matches, but the potential for intentional copying seems less convincing in the face of other metrics. No marked segment had more than two sentences from a single source, and many of the marked segments were essentially meaningless word combinations. One of the segments from the source with the most hits is: "have a long history of … in this manner … To our knowledge, our work … marks the first … specifically for." A non-native English speaker could well have looked for examples of how to formulate a correct sentence and borrowed sequences like this, where it would be possible to fill in more specific words that fit the content of the article. In fact, the author of this work appears from the origin to be a native speaker of another language. Despite iThenticate's reported high percentage of matches, the other metrics tell a different story, especially given the number of disparate sources and the gaps in most marked passages that separate standard phrases from words that express the content of the article. If deliberate copying took place, it seems more likely to have had more to do with the goal of getting expressions right in English than with the content of the paper.

The more serious problem with this article may not be plagiarism, but falsification. Sources that are obscure or hard to find are one indication. Eight of the seventeen references come from the proceedings of conferences. The failure to find proceedings in WorldCat or in Google is no proof that they are fake, because bibliographic control over proceedings is far from perfect, but too many undiscoverable sources build a case against veracity.

3.3.3   EXAMPLE 2

This article was also submitted to a social science-oriented journal, and demonstrates different problems than Example 1. Like the previous article it is short, with under 3,000 words. iThenticate finds 29 matches from 12 sources for a similarity figure of 28%, excluding bibliography and quotes. Most of the matches come in larger blocks in the first few paragraphs. Table 3.2 is shorter and tells a different story.

This somewhat longer article has more marked passages and ones that are more contiguous. The article also has no sentences where the matches came from multiple sources. In the beginning paragraphs, there is one block of ten contiguous marked sentences, and later a block of 13 sentences, after which most of the marked sentences are single instances. This looks more like

Table 3.2: Sentences marked as matches in Example 2

Contiguous Sentences	Source(s)
3 sentences	unmarked
10 sentences	3 sources
6 sentences	unmarked
1 sentence	1 source
13 sentences	4 sources
1 sentence	1 source
2 sentences	2 sources
3 sentences	unmarked
1 sentence	1 source
2 sentences	1 source
25 sentences	unmarked
1 sentence	1 source
4 sentences	unmarked
1 sentence	1 source
3 sentences	unmarked
1 sentence	1 source
4 sentences	unmarked
2 sentences	2 sources
19 sentences	unmarked
1 sentence	1 source
8 sentences	unmarked
1 sentence	1 source
2 sentences	unmarked
2 sentences	1 source
5 sentences	unmarked

classic plagiarism, where an author uses large sections of text from other works. One large block of four sentences early in the work has a reference to "Google, 2011," with no more specifics in the list of references at the end. iThenticate points to a source at "conferences.alia.org.au." The actual source is "http://conferences.alia.org.au/alia2012/Papers/2_Sarah.Schindeler.pdf" and the passage itself contains the Google reference, with the difference that the references in the original source expand on the cryptic Google reference:

> "Google. (2011). The Mobile Movement report. Available from http://www.gstatic.com/ads/research/en/2011_TheMobileMovement.pdf" (Schindeler, 2012)

One reference in the article matches a source that iThenticate found, but the phrase that iThenticate marked, "contact information and even location information," is so generic that the author could easily have reproduced it without intending to plagiarize. The article itself has no direct references to its own literature list and has no passages with quotation marks. The references in the literature list appear to be genuine after some spot checking.

Aside from the two contiguous blocks, which alone could be strong indications of plagiarism, there are only weak indications of intentional copying. iThenticate tends to be zealous in its detection algorithm and often picks up phrases that are perhaps not standard usage, but so anodyne that only within the context of articles on the same topic could there be any reasonable suspicion of plagiarism. Nonetheless iThenticate also finds four whole sentences outside of the larger blocks that match other articles. Partial sentences could suggest an attempt at rewriting content, but whole sentences are harder to attribute to accident.

Example 3

The dissertation by the former defense minister Karl-Theodor Freiherr zu Guttenberg can be discussed without anonymization, since the accusations have been very public. The title puts the work clearly in the area of political science: "Verfassung und Verfassungsvertrag. Konstitutionelle Entwicklungsstufen in den U.S. und der EU" [Constitution and Constitutional Agreements. Constitutional development stages in the U.S. and the EU] The statistics on the GuttenPlag website are somewhat more detailed than on VroniPlag: 1,218 plagiarism fragments were found in 135 sources. This includes 371 of the 393 pages (94%) and 10,421 lines (63.8%) [GuttenPlag-Anonymous, 2011]. This was the first case that the group of plagiarism-hunters addressed, who later formed VroniPlag, and the evidence of plagiarism seemed overwhelming. The blocks of copied text were large. Some were slightly rewritten, but with so few word changes that the original sentence was easy to recognize. Standard phrases appear, but in a context where chance seems unlikely.

This case raises questions about when the evidence of plagiarism becomes so overwhelming that detailed metrics are unnecessary. While making hasty assumptions can be risky, this case offers numerous examples of large blocks of contiguous text with no references, no quotation marks, and no apparent attempt at rewriting. If 50% of the text had such problems, there would be little doubt that the author intended deception. If 5% of a long text such as this had that kind of match, it would be about 20 pages, and that could reasonably be seen as going over an implicit limit, even though the percentage is small. If the amount were 1% (about 4 pages), it may still count as evidence of some intention to deceive because of the large number of contiguous words (roughly 1,000). If the matching only involved that portion of the work where the author was intentionally reporting on the contributions of others, such as the literature review, evaluators might want to consider whether the matches sufficiently undermined the ultimate scholarly value of the whole to justify drastic punishments. Metrics help, even very simple metrics, but in the end someone must balance the putative plagiarism against the overall value of the work.

3.4   IN THE NATURAL SCIENCES

3.4.1   OVERVIEW

Plagiarism in the natural sciences is no less of a concern than in the humanities and the social sciences, but the natural sciences in general put less value on the originality of expression, since verbal inputs and verbal analysis play a secondary role to the data and the analysis. The data tend to be numerical, but are by no means exclusively so, and the analyses tend also to be mathematical or at least to involve a range of methods that follow a strong formal logic. Physics is a classic example of a highly mathematical field where the data tend to be numeric and the quantitative analysis relies on complex formulas. When two physicists measure the same natural phenomenon, the goal is not originality, but consistency, and when one physicist makes a slight change to improve the formula that another used, it is not copying or paraphrasing but genuine scientific innovation. A reference to the past formula would be normal, but quotation marks around the original would be odd.

Retraction Watch categorizes the retractions it follows by subject. Out of 332 retractions listed in Retraction Watch from December 2010 through May 2016, 93 fit their physics category (28%). Of these 93, ten were considered plagiarism (11%), one was self-plagiarism, and five (5%) were largely or entirely duplication of a whole paper in a different journal. This adds up to 16 out of the 93 physics papers (17%). Considering the total number of physics publications, these amounts are small. It is worth noting that Retraction Watch focuses on formal retractions in journals. It is unclear how many physics papers that appeared in the ArXiv open access repository at Cornell, or at other open access repositories, may never have reached formal publication because readers discovered plagiarism problems. This form of filter likely produced some withdrawals when the problems were exposed. The ArXiv covers a wide range of mathematical subjects, including "Physics, Mathematics, Computer Science, Quantitative Biology, Quantitative Finance and Statistics" (ArXiv.org, 2016). It is likely that the potential filtering effect catches some plagiarism in these other fields too. That is a topic for future research.

The subject boundaries of the natural sciences are clear only at the extremes. Physics, chemistry, and astronomy clearly belong, and mathematics, computer science, and geology are virtually always in that category. Biology and medicine may be classified as natural sciences, or they may be part of a new category (perhaps a sub-category) called "life sciences." The life sciences differ in having less of a pure laboratory focus and using more field-based observation so that they tend to resemble some social sciences in being verbal. Psychology may belong to the life sciences. Depending on the time and place, it has also belonged to the social sciences, or (much earlier) even to the humanities. This monograph will treat it as a natural science because of the role laboratory work plays in modern psychology research.

Engineering in all of its forms is typically a category unto itself, but it can belong to the natural sciences, since it is generally more intensely mathematical than the average social science. Retraction Watch currently lists engineering separately with the relatively modest number of 59 retractions, some of which overlap with physics. Of the 59 retractions, 12 (20%) were for plagiarism and 8 (13.6%) were for duplication. Both for plagiarism and for duplication (that is, publishing in two different journals), these figures are roughly double those for physics, which could be some small additional evidence that prior exposure in a repository could filter out plagiarism problems.

One of the notable features of natural science and engineering publications is the amount of co-authorship. The journal *Nature* reports a "physics paper with 5,154 authors" [Castelvecchi, 2015]. While this is reputedly a record number, it is not unusual for whole lab groups to be listed, both as a standard courtesy within the discipline, and because large-scale physics or engineering or other projects often involve many people, who do some part of the data collection or the data analysis or write some portion of the text. The number of multi-authored retractions is not trivial: for only the month of May 2016, Retraction Watch shows 22 retractions for multi-authored papers and just four for papers with a single author. The numbers show the predominance of multiple-authorship in contemporary scholarly publishing. Not all of these retractions had to do with plagiarism, but all involved either natural science or social science topics.

Large numbers of authors could open the risk for more plagiarism, or they could reduce it because more people are looking at the text. That is hard to determine. Nonetheless it increases the importance of an analysis whose metrics locate the problem specifically, so that an attempt could be made to assess responsibility. In theory the main author or authors ought to have checked the work thoroughly, but in practice they may be guilty of no worse a crime than a misplaced trust in one of their co-workers.

3.4.2   EXAMPLE 1

This example comes from agricultural science. Since the accusation has been published in a German newspaper, the case is by no means secret. Nonetheless this monograph will refer to the author as "TB" rather than by name to avoid any potential for further ongoing damage to his reputation. Those who want to know the name may look at the references under Fischer [2016].

The actual accusations are anonymous, since the name of the accuser appears neither in the summary of the accusations in the Ostsee newspaper, nor in the detailed page-by-page listing. The accuser has explicitly taken VroniPlag as a model, but it is not clear to what degree the accuser adheres to VroniPlag's standards and guidelines. A summary of the accusation says:

"Von den 66 Textseiten sind bislang auf 44 Seiten ungekennzeichnete Übernahmen aus anderen Texten festzustellen (= 67% der Textseiten). Für weitere Seiten (z. B. S. 13 und 14) bestehen Verdachtsmomente, da hier keinerlei Quellenangaben getätigt wurden. Auf mind. 14 Seiten sind mehr als 50 Prozent des Textes betroffen. Zudem wurde eine Karte der Klimaregionen (S. 98) ohne Quellenbeleg Übernommen. Insgesamt wurden bislang mehr als 300 Einzelstellen mit Plagiaten festgestellt." [Ostsee Zeitung anonymous writer, 2016]

[Of the 66 pages of text there are 44 pages with unreferenced passages from other sources (=67% of the pages of text). Other pages (e.g., 13 and 14) are suspect because they offer no sources. On at least 14 pages over 50 percent of the text was affected. In addition a map of the climate regions (p. 98) was taken with no source attribution. In total so far there are more than 300 individual places where plagiarism has been established.] [author's translation]

Taken at its face value, the accusation appears systematic and conclusive. If these figures are true, the accusation of plagiarism could well be justified, but accusations are easy to make and eager plagiarism hunters are sometimes careless, especially when writing anonymously. A grayscale analysis offers the chance to distinguish between types of accusations. An analysis has been done using categories for texts with no references (see Table 3.3) and for texts with a reference (see Table 3.4).

The results of the grayscale analysis cannot be given in detail, because they could potentially be part of official investigations, and the results are not really important for this lecture except as examples that show how the grayscale analysis works.

An example of a phrase that was marked as copied (plagiarized), but could reasonably count as general knowledge is on p. 9 of the work[3]: "Mecklenburg-Vorpommern ist dem 03.10.1990 das nordostlichste Bundesland Deutschlands." [Mecklenburg-Vorpommern is the most north-easterly state of Germany since 03 October 1990.] The accusation is that the source comes from p. 5 of a work by K. Billwitz et al., "Historischer und geographischer Atlas von Mecklenburg und Pommern" that was published in 1995. The same general information does appear in Billwitz, but not in that exact formulation. Even if Billwitz used the same exact formulation, the information is so plainly factual that almost anyone could invent the same sentence.

An example of a marked sentence with a degree of similarity is on p. 35 of the dissertation:

"In der Regel beträgt die standort- und sortenbedingte Spanne für die Aussaatmenge **130 bis 160 kg/ha**." [In general the local and type-specific range for the amount of sowing is 130 to 160 kg/ha.]

The sentence in the putative source reads:

"Die derzeitig in Anwendung kommende Saatmenge beträgt für unsere Roggengegenden mit nicht zu leichtem Boden **130-160 kg/ha** bei Drill- und 150-190 kg/ha bei Breitsaat." (Becker-Dillingen, 1927, "Handbuch des Gesammten Pflanzenbaues," p. 156) [The current seed quantity for rye fields with not very light soil is 150–190 kg/ha with a seed drill and 130–160 kg/ha with broadcast seeding.]

---

[3]The accusation in Fischer [2016] links to the dissertation.

Table 3.3: Plagiarism grayscale metrics for texts with a reference

Name	Description	Label	Valuation
Significant matches	Multiple identical sentences in a paragraph	C1	Probable plagiarism
Some matches 1	More tha 5 contiguous words within a sentence of more than 5 words	C2	Potential plagiarism
Some matches 2	More than 3 exact phrases of more than 3 words overlap in contiguous sentences in a paragraph	C3	Potential plagiarism
Some matches 3	Fewer than 5 contiguous words within a sentence of more than 5 words	C4	Potential plagiarism
Similarity 1	fewer than 3 exact phrases of more than 3 words overlap in contiuous sentences in a paragraph of more than 9 words in sequence	S1	Questionable practice
Similarity 2	More than 5 of the exact same words (excluding function words) in contiguous sentences in the same paragraph	S2	Questionable practice
Topic overlap	Shared facts and standard phrases	S3	Probably not plagiarism
Standard words	Widely used words of phrases in this context	SW	Not plagiarism
General knowledge	Information so broadly known that formulations cannot be considered unique	GK	Not plagiarism
Implied quotation	Something such as an indentation or colon implies that the passage was quoted, but no reference is supplied	IQ	Matching without an intent to deceive

There are very few contiguous words in common between the two sentences, mainly the amount "130–160 kg/ha." The author does not say where the figures come from, but figures about how much seed to plant may have more than one source. There is some similarity in the structure of the sentence, but that could be unsurprising given the context.

The following example shows a greater overlap in words. The duplicate words have been marked in bold:

"Er **hüfelte**, und so **stehen seine Pflanzen auf Dämmen**. Das Häufeln musste **2mal im Herbst** erfolgen. Wegen des hohen Arbeitsaufwandes war diese Methode

Table 3.4: Plagiarism grayscale metrics for texts with a reference

Name	Description	Label	Valuation
Missing quotes	A correct reference is there but the quotation marks are missing	MQ	Bad practice, but no deception
Incomplete reference	A partial reference is there, but quotation marks are missing	IR	Bad practice, probably no deception
Bad reference	An inaccurate reference is there, with or without quotation marks	BR	Bad practice, potential deception

nicht praktikabel. Hinzu kamen pflanzenbauliche Wirkungen, die sich z. T. negativ auswirkten, insbesondere in Trockenjahren." [TB, 2001, p. 38]

"DEMTSCHINSKY **häufelte** an. **Seine Pflanzen stehen** also **auf Dämmen**. Es verlangt eine möglichst fröhzeitige und dünne Saat mit nachfolgender ein- bis **zweimaliger** Anhüufelung **im Herbst**, damit die Pflanzen möglichst kräftig in den Winter kommen." [Becker-Dillingen, 1929, p. 50]

A translation would show the same general topic, but would disguise the word order, which is important here because it is not exactly the same. The word order could easily have been rearranged in an attempt to disguise, but the fact that both authors are discussing practical aspects of when to plant under the same conditions in the same region, the possibility exists that they used nine of the same words to discuss the same subject.

Not all examples are equally innocent. In the following quote, the exact passage can be found in an article from a century earlier.

"Das Sickerwasser schwemmt allmählich die feinsten Partikel des Bodens in die Tiefe und veranlasst dadurch eine Verarmung der oberen und eine Bereicherung der unteren Bodenschichten an diesen Bestandteilen" [TB, 2001, p. 35].

"Das Sickerwasser schwemmt allmählich die feinsten Partikel in die Tiefe und veranlasst dadurch eine Verarmung der oberen und eine Bereicherung der unteren Bodenschichten an diesen Bestandtheilen." [Wollny, 1896, p. 384]

[The seepage carries the finest particles of the soil into the depths and causes an impoverishment of the upper and an enrichment of the lower levels of the soil in these components.]

The context here is important. The phrase before the passage in TB is:

"Das Hauptargument für die Pflugarbeit war:" [The main argument for the ploughing was:]

The colon could reasonably suggest a quoted passage, and a reader should expect some form of reference at this point. There is none, but the sentence immediately afterward implies that this could be a reference to the literature:

> "In der Literatur sind zahlreiche Arbeiten über die negativen Auswirkungen der wuh-lenden Bodenbearbeitung zu finden." [In the literature many examples of the negative effects of turning the soil can be found.] [TB, 2001]

The lack of a reference is a serious error, but the implied quotation could also suggest possible laziness on the part of the author rather than a real attempt to deceive. The phrase also describes a factual and technical situation. Too many contiguous words are identical for the passage to be chance, but they could well come from notes that a student made during a lecture. For plagiarism-hunters this is no excuse, but it could also be judged to be bad practice rather than malpractice.

The era in which this doctoral dissertation was written is potentially relevant. The author studied mainly during the years of the German Democratic Republic, when international con-tact and interaction with international standards was politically limited. This is not an excuse for intentional deception, but it may suggest a working environment in which the recognition of the intellectual property rights of others may have been treated with greater laxity than is true today. A balanced judgment about malpractice may not satisfy self-appointed vigilantes, but should have the goal of coming closer to the truth about the author's intentions.

3.4.3   EXAMPLE 2

Medicine belongs broadly to the natural sciences, and medicine is an area with large numbers of retractions, many of which are for plagiarism. Retraction Watch lists 1,024 retractions for "clinical studies" as of 31 May 2016, the prestigious journal *Lancet* had 15 and the *New England Journal of Medicine* (listed as NEJM) had 17. The U.S. Office of Research Integrity has a mission by law to "make proposed findings of research misconduct and administrative actions in response to allegations of research misconduct involving research conducted or supported by components of the Public Health Service…" [Office of Research Integrity, 2014]. Medical degrees account for 106 of the 171 entries in VroniPlag (62%). This is not necessarily a sign that medical research is more corrupt than other forms of research. Public institutions and those who hunt integrity violations may focus more on medical research because flawed studies in medicine can have direct negative consequences for the public.

A case that is public because dissertations in Germany must be published and because VroniPlag has published its accusations is "Die Analyze der hepatischen Mikrozirkulation nach IIschämie und Reperfusion während der humanen Lebertransplantation" [The analysis of hepatic microcirculation after ischemia and reperfusion during human liver transplants]. As usual in this lecture, the author's name will not be given in the text, only the abbreviation that VroniPlag uses: "GDP." A full reference can be found in the literature list.

VroniPlag gives the following statistics: plagiarism has been documented on 33 out of the 88 pages, which is 37.5% of all pages. Nine pages have 50%–75% matching text, and nine have over 75%. Using the color markings to get a percentage that reflects the number of matches in the text rather than just the number of pages with matches, the figures are between 26.4% (taking the colors at maximum value) and 20.4% (using the color midpoints where red is 87%, maroon is 62.5%, and black is 30%). A look through all of the marked pages shows that the matches all came from a single source, including the footnotes. A curious feature of the matching is that the references often expand the list of co-authors from a single primary author "et al." to at least three primary authors "et al."

Arguably this deviation from simple copying has to do with either the university's or the doctoral advisor's requirements for how references are done, rather than with an attempt to disguise the copying. The mass of copying from a single source makes this an unusual case. Nonetheless a metric worth noting is that a portion of the matched text consists of references in footnotes. On p. 85, for example, the footnote section is 42% of the marked text. On the following page it is 66% percent. While copying footnotes references in this context from a single source is still arguably plagiarism, a fair metric should recognize that the amount of marked text (as opposed to references) is significantly smaller.

3.5 CONCLUSION: PLAGIARISM

There are too many plagiarism cases of different types and varying circumstances to argue that the few cases that were analyzed above constitute a representative sample of plagiarism. They were chosen deliberately to demonstrate certain kinds of metrics. Many plagiarism systems give a standard set of metrics, often the number of pages with plagiarism and a percentage that variously represents the amount of matching on pages, lines, or sentences. The higher the granularity, the more accurate the percentage, but it is rare that a single number tells the whole story.

The most recent medical example above shows how a percentage system can give an inaccurate result when it counts references as if they belong to the text. References can, of course, be copied, even plagiarized, but no one expects originality from a reference. A good reference is supposed to reproduce the names, titles, and publisher information. References represent an element of an academic work whose purpose is largely orthogonal to originality. Their whole purpose is to indicate what content comes from elsewhere. iThenticate allows editors to set a default that excludes references from the percentage total. Not all systems do.

References are just one aspect of the intellectual context within the overall structure of a work. Not all parts of the text of an academic work pretend to equal originality. The introduction to a work ideally explains why the topic is important, and that importance generally builds on ideas that are current within the discipline. The literature review section explicitly does not aim at originality, but at recapitulating the state of the discourse in the field and on the topic. Taking exact expressions from others without explicit quotes fits the definition of plagiarism, but may on balance not vitiate the overall scholarly contribution, if the arguments at the core of the work are in fact original—except perhaps in those fields that view any amount of plagiarism as fatal.

The discipline itself is a part of the context that makes a difference in how to judge instances of plagiarism, and generally this varies with the role the quality of the writing plays in the valuation of a work. For the humanities, words matter. They are both the input data and the means of analysis. A stolen word is a stolen thought. In the more mathematical sciences, however, the words are hardly more than a necessary framework for presenting the real (numeric) data and the mathematical logic that represent the real analysis. Symbols matter more than words in this environment. The symbols are shared, but changes in their arrangement provide originality.

Measurements of the amount of matching in a text can use a range of units. Larger units of measure mask information about context. Small units may focus too much on problem areas without putting them in relation to other parts. The number of contiguous words and the number of identical words matter, as does the likelihood that a phrase is so common that a reasonable chance exists that it occurred to two authors simultaneously. The goal of this chapter is by no means to excuse plagiarism, but to put plagiarism cases in a grayscale context where editors, reviewers, and university commissions can make more informed judgments based on more precise metrics.

CHAPTER 4

Quantifying Data Falsification

4.1 INTRODUCTION

Data falsification is in some sense the mirror image of plagiarism. Plagiarism is a problem that comes from a lack of creativity—copying the expression of others—while data falsification comes from an excess of creativity—creating data to produce particular results. Genuine research data may be unique in the sense that no one else has produced them before, but an important goal in the sciences and social sciences is that results, and therefore the data, be reproducible. There may be legal questions about whether the process that produces a particular result has been patented and thus protected, but data in and of themselves have no legal protection in the U.S.[1] The European Union protects data only when "arranged in a systematic or methodical way" [WIPO, 1997, 1997].

Data in general consist of three parts: the provenance, which explains where they came from and may be in narrative form; the description, which may take the form of metadata; and the data themselves, which can be numeric or textual or multimedia—images specifically will be discussed in the next chapter. Falsification can occur in any of these parts. In the first two sections of this chapter on the humanities and the social sciences, the discussion will focus on provenance issues involving fraudulent data. Data manipulation is possible in these areas too, but more focus will be put on that in the final section on the natural sciences.

Research data are almost by definition a product of a set of processes that researchers may copy and use as intermediate results or may analyze in order to draw conclusions. It is considered appropriate today to give a reference when taking data from others, and sharing or reusing large amounts of data is normal and proper in many fields. Physics is known for sharing very large datasets from experiments at institutions like CERN, where there is general agreement that no one person is likely to be able to analyze the whole stream of results. Astronomy is another area with very large sets of data that come from space exploration programs.

The sharing phenomenon is not limited to the natural sciences. Researchers in finance, for example, use the CRSP (Center for Research in Security Prices) database and people doing bibliometrics share the Web of Science database. Reliability is one of the hallmarks of good data and these shared data sets are generally high quality and well described. In general researchers can rightly assume that they are free from manipulation, with some caveats.[2] The data sets are essentially elements of the research infrastructure, much as are operating systems and networks.

---

[1]See Feist,1991 [1991].
[2]See Section 4.4.5, Database Revisions.

Large datasets are the exception, however, and have the disadvantage of limiting what a researcher can study to common topics.

The extent to which new research builds on past results is not always clear, even when theory suggests that this process should be true over time. Often these past data are just not available to other researchers. One reason is that many owners do not share their data because they worry that someone will take it and use it to make competing discoveries. Another reason is that data may be shared privately within relatively closed communities, but not exposed publicly. And a third reason can be that the research data were uploaded to a publicly accessible repository, but are not readily discoverable for any of a range of causes including searcher ignorance or sharing problems with the repository.

When data are not available, researchers must either trust past published results, or they must recreate the data as best they can based on descriptions in the published works, which often turn out to be too cryptic. This unclarity has consequences. As a computer scientist said in a recent private conversation, publications are just "advertisements" for the actual research.[3] Descriptions are no substitute for the data itself.

The problems inherent in recreating data (and the costs involved) are among the reasons for the contemporary push to make research data more available and more reusable. Publicaly available data increase the transparency of past research by allowing researchers to do more than just reuse them. They can also use the data as a comparison set when trying to repeat an experiment. Parts of the data may also be useful when researchers want to make modifications in an experiment that affects only certain aspects. Where researchers share data, false data build in errors that can mislead the direction of research, but sharing can also help to discover errors in datasets. Exposing data does not guarantee reliability, but it helps.

4.2 METADATA

Data can take many forms in the various disciplines, as will be discussed later in this chapter, and some forms are more transparent in their meaning than others. It is a rule of thumb in research data that some form of metadata are needed to make the individual fields and sequences within a data stream clear. Falsifying metadata is not a common research integrity issue, but anyone who has worked extensively with the metadata descriptions of complex data sets knows how imprecise the definitions can be. This is not just a matter of a date format being country-inspecific, but an inherent vagueness based on assumptions that can be wrong. Data from two different machines may not, for example, measure with exactly the same precision or even measure exactly the same spectrum of data. In the social sciences any data that comes from human sources can have a level of variability that belies the apparent precision of an exact definition. What this means is that a certain amount of data cleaning (manipulation) may be necessary. In good research practice any such cleaning is documented so that it is transparent. Imperfect documentation is a problem, but may only represent carelessness, not deception.

---

[3]Conversation with Steven Griffin in Berlin, September 09, 2016.

Mislabeling or misrepresenting the meaning or the precision of a data field in research can be as damaging as falsifying the data themselves, because it presents the information as something other than it is. The mislabeling can be inadvertent, as when a survey asks a question where the researcher makes assumptions about how the respondents understand the question. When asking respondents about types of publication, for example, a researcher cannot be sure that the respondents have the same definition in mind, even if a definition were given as part of the question. Respondents' own ideas may reshape what they read, depending on their prior assumptions and the community they belong to. Knowing exactly what research data truly represent is hard, even with the best of effort.

Standards for citing data are poorly established, except in the humanities, where the data mainly only involve text. One reason for the lack of standards may be an expectation that people are creating original research data for their own exclusive use, and that, while some description is necessary, a citation is not. Today there is an emphasis on making research data public so that others can reuse it. Data that have not been properly and fully described are not false per se, but they can lead to false conclusions. Fear [2013] wrote about the complexity of this kind of documentation for certain highly technical fields in her dissertation at the University of Michigan:

> "Since microarray data require a more complex metadata structure than gene sequence data to make them understandable and usable by others, scientists have to do more work to make them shareable and thus they are shared less often." [p. 19]

The barriers are not merely the complexity of the information. The willingness to take the time to prepare a complete description is often lacking, as she notes further in her dissertation:

> "However, other fields have found barriers to this kind of comprehensive metadata creation process: researchers can be resistant to spending additional time and effort to create their own metadata, and researchers can also be unprepared to address issues such as intellectual property concerns, privacy, and concerns over data quality (Mathys & Kamel Boulos, 2011)." [Fear, 2013, p. 22]

A general unwillingness to describe research data accurately and extensively is not a sign of potential falsification, but it can be a warning signal. It may be that those who falsify data in fact do not take the trouble to invent detailed descriptions of the structure and origins of the data. James Hunton, an accounting researcher whose papers have mostly been retracted, reputedly told co-authors that he had signed confidentiality agreements with his sources. He may even have fabricated some documentation as evidence.[4] This was enough to convince well known co-authors that his data were genuine. In many scientific and scholarly fields, getting access to fresh and relevant data is sometimes as important as writing up the analysis. Nonetheless the academic world gives little credit for creating a valuable and easily reusable dataset, and simplifying the process of data gathering through invention is a temptation. There is as yet no evidence that giving

---

[4]See Section 4.4.4, James Hunton.

appropriate academic credit to the creation of reusable data sets would reduce the temptation to falsify data, but there is at least a reasonable chance that it would help.

Publicly accessible research data repositories take a variety of forms and repositories often require some form of formal metadata. The German Research Foundation, which sponsored project re3data [2016] writes: "re3data.org has reached a milestone of identifying and listing 1,500 research data repositories…" including 249 archives in Germany and 805 in the U.S. as of April 2016. The range of metadata types is extremely broad. Dublin Core metadata accounts for the largest number with 69 followed closely by ISO19115 with 62.

The benefit of Dublin Core metadata is that its fifteen-element structure is so simple that essentially anyone can fill in the fields. Its weakness is that the rules and definitions are so flexible that precision is often missing. Dublin Core works well for conventional text-based bibliographic content, but only one element, "description," is really available for a detailed breakdown of the structure of the bitstream of research data. ISO 19115 is a standard for geographic information systems that offers more specific elements and has variations such as a related marine metadata framework that uses semantic web technologies. The greater specificity helps, but does not guarantee that people have filled out the metadata correctly.

4.3   HUMANITIES

4.3.1   INTRODUCTION

Data in the humanities generally means text. There are disciplines in the humanities that use quantitative data—historians, for example, who pursue economic history and practice "Cliometrics"—but their methods resemble the social sciences and will be discussed in that section. Although humanists do not always think of the contents of books and journals and archives as data in the same way that the social and natural scientists use the word data, this monograph will refer to the verbal content of these sources as "data" because it serves as input to humanities research in much the same way that the results from a survey are data for a social scientist or the numeric readings from a machine represent data for a natural scientist.

Retraction Watch has very few examples of humanities retractions that are not plagiarism-related. An example comes from the *Guardian* on March 1st, 2016, in an article entitled, "The Human-animal studies academics dogged by German hoaxers," by Philip Oltermann [2016]. The original study was a deliberate fake:

> "… the editorial team at the Hannah-Arendt Institute for Research into Totalitarianism said they had been 'systematically deceived, i.e., through a faked CV and an apparently academic argumentation, which sought to convince the reader with detailed explanations, extensive footnotes and false archival references.' Christiane Schulte did not exist, and nor did the alsatians with totalitarian tendencies."

This was certainly data falsification, even if it were intended as a hoax. The fact that it was a hoax ultimately made it easier to discover:

"The academics behind the hoax wrote they had deliberately included details that could have got them found out, such as naming the dog shot near the Berlin Wall as 'Rex'—the name of a police dog in an Austrian TV show popular in Germany, Kommissar Rex—or suggesting that the planned memorial for the victims of the wall should also include a symbolic dog lead made of steel. 'At that point at the latest we had expected objections, doubt or protest. Instead we got applause,' they said."

If a deliberate hoax is that hard to discover, it is not surprising that genuine data falsification often goes without detection.

There is a broad-scale expectation among humanities students and even scholars that the published works in a respectable research library represent a reliable core of information. Reliable in this case does not mean perfect or complete, only that the publishers and the libraries make an active effort to cull out dubious claims and dubious titles. Humanists at top institutions are generally conscious of quality differences among publishers. Books from publishers like the University of Chicago Press or the Oxford University Press have more weight and prestige than from a relatively unknown publisher that draws authors primarily from people who must publish. Books from a less prestigious publisher may be every bit as well researched and correct as those from better known sources, but a semi-conscious tendency exists to treat them as potentially more suspect, even if the only difference is the relative breadth or narrowness of the topic.

In the 1970s the *Journal of Modern History* did an experiment where good articles on topics of less broad interest were published only as abstracts in the journal and could be requested by those who wanted to read them. One reason for the experiment's failure was a sense that the abstracts-only articles were second class, even though the reviewing was the same and the editors said that breadth of interest was the only factor. The point is that humanists are ready to make quality judgments, even without a hint of suggestion that the data are imperfect. An important metric for them is publisher ranking.

Discovering falsification in humanities data is hard, which may be one reason why humanities scholars rely on publishers to do the work of weeding out dubious works, but publishers are also poorly equipped for the task. The most reliable way to check the genuineness of historical data, for example, is to go back to the original sources. That should be possible for data that come from archives, if the archive is publicly available. In a paper world, a thorough review of such sources takes time and expense. It could mean traveling to the archive in question and essentially repeating the author's work to check on whether the facts were correct. Publishers may and often do check controversial or surprising facts, but the kind of automated checking that is possible with plagiarism is largely unavailable for humanities data today. A problem is that too many archives are still only in paper form, which automated processes cannot check until systematic digitization takes place, and that is some years off, especially for hand-written materials.

Another problem in discovering falsification in humanist data is that the data are a mix of facts and personal interpretation. The interpretation not only involves selection and inclusion, but shades of meaning for the information content itself. All disciplines include an analysis component, but in the humanities it is often more difficult to separate "pure" facts from the author's impression of what those facts are saying. Simple factual errors are relatively easy to catch, and were often caught in pre-digital times, but separating fact from selection and analysis is harder because it is often presented less explicitly. With data from an archive, for example, a historian may legitimately gather facts about demographic mobility without including facts about mortality, because those facts seem less relevant to the specific argument the historian wants to make. This would not be considered falsification under normal circumstances, but could be if mobility and mortality were closely intertwined in a particular location, during a plague, for example. In other words, many cases are judgment calls with relatively little explicit evidence. Plausibility or doubt is what often decides a case.

The following sections will look at humanities data falsification in specific disciplines.

4.3.2   HISTORY

A data falsification case that came to public attention in the 1980s was the "Hitler Diaries." The diaries appeared in the form of hand-written notebooks that were "written at great speed by Konrad Kujau, a small-time crook and prolific forger" [McGrane, 2013]. What is interesting from the perspective of this monograph is the relative crudeness of the forgery and the damage done to scholars, especially the noted Oxford historian Hugh Trevor-Roper, and "his awful humiliation in the matter of the Hitler diaries" [Ascherson, 2010a]. Trevor-Roper first declared the diaries to be genuine and then began backing away. Robert McFadden [1983] wrote in the *New York Times*:

> "The chief claim for authenticity came from Mr. Trevor-Roper. In an article in The Times of London on Saturday, he wrote that he had inspected many of the documents in the vault of a Swiss bank and had come away convinced they were genuine. Yesterday, however, he was quoted by Reuters as saying he still had some nagging doubts because there had never been any previous hint of the diaries' existence."

When a set of physical tests were done on the paper on which the diaries were written, the evidence for forgery became clear. J. Grant [1985] carried out the physical tests and wrote:

> "The fluorescent areas contained rag pulp, indicating the addition (re-use) of waste paper of a higher grade than the remainder of the fibrous matter. This is a common practice in paper making. The fluorescence was derived from this latter constituent, and qualitative tests showed it to be due to the presence in the re-used paper of an optical brightening agent. These agents were not used in paper making in Germany during Adolf Hitler's lifetime." [p. 189]

Ascherson [2010b] explains how Trevor-Roper could have mistaken a crude forgery for something genuine, especially in an area where he was considered a leading expert:

> "The omens are easy to pick out. Trevor-Roper, although he had seen plenty of forgeries (some of Kersten's Nazi 'archives,' for instance), grew dangerously confident that

he could identify a fake. And he could be perversely uncritical when on a research trail that excited him."

This story highlights the methodological problems with data falsification in the humanities. If a forger is as uninformed as Konrad Kujau, it is relatively easy to perform physical tests on the paper and ink to prove that they are from a different era, but more sophisticated forgers can get older paper and period-authentic ink sources. Handwriting can also be imitated. An even more effective way to create a forgery might be to provide a transcript with only small fragments of an original that was supposedly burned or otherwise damaged and not easily tested. Kujau did not do this because he was in a hurry and he wanted to sell the original diaries as artifacts, which garnered far more cash than a mere transcript would have. A transcript could, however, have been harder to disprove precisely because, as in the case of Hugh Trevor-Roper, judgments about authenticity in the humanities often involve plausibility, and a strong desire for something like new sources on a hot topic can cloud even ordinarily reliable minds.

Trevor-Roper did not lose his professorship because of this instance of poor judgment, but the damage to his reputation was lasting.

4.3.3   ART AND ART HISTORY

Some of the same kinds of forgery problems occur in art, especially involving paintings by famous artists where large amounts of money can be at stake. The forgeries can also affect the scholarly discourse in art history. A notable recent story is the forgery of a set of Galileo watercolors of the moon in a work called "Sidereus Nuncius." The work was enormously important, especially for the illustrations that accompanied the text. The original was produced in a small run. Nicholas Schmidle [2013] describes the situation when two Italians brought a new copy to a well-respected bookseller named Richard Lan, who had ties to Owen Gingrich, a leading expert on Galileo:

> "Lan had viewed many copies of the 'Sidereus Nuncius' over the years. Although some had been in better condition, none contained the personal flourishes of this one. Galileo's signature was on the title page. A stamp of a lynx indicated that the book came from the personal library of Federico Cesi, the founder of the Accademia dei Lincei, the scientific fraternity in Rome to which Galileo belonged. Instead of etchings, there were five lovely watercolor illustrations of the moon, presumably painted by Galileo. Lan suspected that the book would sell for millions of dollars, once he had established its provenance and authenticity."

Gingrich made the first confirmation of the work's authenticity:

> "Soon after the meeting, Gingrich wrote to Lan that there was 'a firm Galileo connection.' He added, 'The drawings had either to be made by Galileo himself or with his supervision.' " [Schmidle, 2013]

Lan was cautious and asked another expert, Horst Bredekamp at Humboldt-Universität zu Berlin, who also confirmed the authenticity:

> "That November [2005], Lan brought his 'Sidereus Nuncius' to Berlin and left it there for a month. As Bredekamp later wrote, after 'a mere glance' at the book he concluded that the splotchy watercolors, with their 'mixture of fidgetiness and precision,' were genuine Galileo sketches. This was a major claim, for it threatened the singularity of a famed set of Galileo drawings known as the Florence Sheet." [Schmidle, 2013]

Bredekamp was not alone in his judgment, and he had the physical work tested as well.

> "The scholars spent two months analyzing Lan's book, using such tools as long-wave ultraviolet radiation (to identify inks) and X-ray fluorescence (to determine the paper's composition). A curator from the Accademia dei Lincei authenticated the lynx stamp, and a conservator from the Staatliche Akademie der Bildenden Künste, in Stuttgart, certified the paper and the binding." [Schmidle, 2013]

The result was a symposium and several books, including Bredekamp [2007] *Galilei der Künstler: der Mond, die Sonne, die Hand* (Akadamie Verlag, 2007), and in 2011 Brückle and Hahn [2011] *Galileo's Sidereus Nuncius: A comparison of the proof copy (New York) with other paradigmatic copies*, edited by Irene Brückle and Oliver Hahn in a series that Horst Bredekamp himself edited. A further volume by Paul Needham followed in 2012: *Galileo Makes a Book: The first edition of Sidereus Nuncius Venice 1610.*

Doubt grew when Nick Wilding from Georgia State University began to have doubts while writing a review. He noticed details that were not quite right, such as small differences in the size of an etching supposedly based on the watercolors. Slowly more evidence for the forgery accumulated.

> "Another researcher discovered cotton linters in the paper stock, which would have required a ginning capability that didn't exist until 1793." [Schmidle, 2013]

Eventually the forgery became clear. In the book *A Galileo Forgery: Unmasking the New York Sidereus Nuncius* (2014), Bredekamp et al. revised their conclusions:

> "One month later, in June 2012, Nick Wilding exchanged information with Paul Needham, arguing that despite all of the evidence the SNML displayed elements of a forgery. … On the one hand nobody denied the logical rigidity of the newly presented facts. On the other hand the conclusion that the SNML was authentic had been founded on such a firm basis that it seemed unimaginable suddenly to change one's mind. Being confronted with this dilemma, it seemed unavoidable but to take up the investigation once again. The condition for reopening the investigation was to have undeniably authentic as well as clearly forged copies at hand in order to compare both the materials as well as the techniques for making the books." [p. 9]

The book's introduction goes on to refer to Schmidle's article in the *New Yorker*, which is quoted above. The forger was apparently an Italian named Marino Massimo De Caro.

"On August 2, 2012, De Caro began confessing his crimes to Melillo ..." [Schmidle, 2013]

The important lesson in this story is not that a well-done forgery fooled a group of experts, but that metrics for measuring this kind of falsified data—images plus text—were seriously inadequate. One problem may be the binary approach: the work is either genuine or fake. In fact there were genuine aspects (the inks and paper, for example) that misled people into regarding the whole as genuine. The history of art forgery offers many examples of well-done works. Among the most famous forgers was Han Van Meegeren, who proved that he was innocent of selling Dutch art treasures to the Nazis by demonstrating how he had forged them himself:

"The trial of Han van Meegeren began on October 29 1947 in Room 4 of the Regional Court in Amsterdam. In order to demonstrate his case, it was arranged that, under police guard before the court, he would paint another 'Vermeer,' Jesus Among the Doctors, using the materials and techniques he had employed for the other forgeries. ... At the end of the trial, the collaboration charges were changed to forgery and Van Meegeren was condemned to one year in confinement ..." [Janson, 2016]

New technology would likely catch some of the techniques that van Meegeren used, but the basic plausibility test that art experts use to detect fake data—in this case, fake paintings—remains vulnerable to the urge to see something new and exciting rather than to measure a work systematically for elements of possible falsification.

4.3.4 ETHNOGRAPHY

While many of the humanities disciplines rely on data that come from libraries or museums, where the institution provides a de facto certification of authenticity, ethnography (sometimes called cultural or social anthropology) uses data that come from direct observation and direct experience. Before the middle of the 20th century, there were no effective recording devices that an ethnographer could take into the field. Tape recorders existed in the 1960s and 1970s, but were large and not readily portable, and tended to be regarded as invasive when interacting with subjects. Data for ethnographers came largely from personal notes, often made some hours after an observation or an interaction with people. Modern ethnographic training emphasizes blending into the environment and being as unobtrusive as possible. That is not always possible, and recording devices and note-taking serve as reminders to subjects that they are being observed. The trade-off between an exact recording and post-interaction note taking can have to do with how emotionally sensitive the situation is and with how much the recording will change behavior.

An ethnographer could easily create false data by making up observations and interviews. That requires an artistic and literary talent equivalent to art forgery or the forgery of old texts, but without the financial incentive of a lucrative market for such works. There is little or no evidence of this kind of data falsification, perhaps because it is not worth doing or because people who become ethnographers tend to be honest, but perhaps also because such falsifications are hard to detect and to expose as long as they pass a certain plausibility test.

Unintentional data falsification is a more common situation, which may be detectable only after long periods once conflicting information becomes available. An example is the work of Margaret Mead in Samoa, where she explored sexuality and the coming of age. Derek Freeman's 1983 book *Margaret Mead and Samoa: The Making and Unmaking of an Anthropological Myth* raised questions about her observations and analysis. Mead's portrait of the free sexual life of Samoan adolescents had a strong attraction for readers in the 1920s. What she observed was a subset of the range of human behaviors that may have left out potential observations that complicated her story. That is, essentially, the view Freeman put forward. The initial reaction against Freeman's book did not dissuade him. In 1999 he published another, even sharper, critique: *The Fateful Hoaxing of Margaret Mead: A Historical Analysis of Her Samoan Research*. Shaw [2001] wrote in his *New York Times* obituary that Freeman's view "gradually won wide—although not complete—acceptance." The criticisms touched directly on Mead's data collection methods:

> "He [Freeman] said Dr. Mead's research and reporting had been hampered by poor preparation, inadequate command of Samoan, a decision to live mostly among white officials rather than among the islanders, an effort to fit two competing research projects into a few months and pressure from her sponsor."

Language represents an especially important ethnographic data collection tool, and to argue that an ethnographer has a poor command of the language of the population under observation suggests that the data are unreliable. Mead was dead before questions about her data arose and thus could not answer the critique. In any case her reputation suffered, and those who had relied on her work have backed away from it.

4.3.5   LITERATURE

As with other humanities disciplines, the most common form of data falsification in literature is forgery in its broadest sense. One example was Lee Israel, the author of a number of genuine biographies, including *Miss Tallulah Bankhead* (1972), *Kilgallen: A Biography of Dorothy Kilgallen* (1979), and *Estee Lauder: Beyond the Magic (An Unauthorized Biography)* (1985), all of which are still available on Amazon. Margalit Fox [2015] wrote in her New York Times obituary: "Lee Israel, a Writer Proudest of Her Literary Forgeries, Dies at 75":

> "In the early 1990s, with her career at a standstill, she became a literary forger, composing and selling hundreds of letters that she said had been written by Edna Ferber, Dorothy Parker, Noël Coward, Lillian Hellman and others. That work, which ended with Ms. Israel's guilty plea in federal court in 1993, was the subject of her fourth and last book, the memoir 'Can You Ever Forgive Me,' published by Simon & Schuster in 2008."

Her forgeries were skilled scholarly works according to Fox [2015]:

"Ms. Israel's criminal career married scholarship, fabrication, forgery and outright theft. Using the research skills she had honed as a writer, she scoured her subjects' memoirs for salient biographical details; their published letters for epistolary style; and their original, archived letters for typing idiosyncrasies. She bought a flock of period typewriters from secondhand shops and, on furtive library visits, tore blank sheets of vintage paper from the backs of old journals."

The forgeries earned small amounts of money, US $50–$100 each (Fox, 2015), and she was proud of them: "Of her body of forgeries, Ms. Israel wrote in her memoir, 'I still consider the letters to be my best work' " [Fox, 2015].

A similar example can be found in the 2008 publication of a poem about the financial crisis that was listed as coming from Kurt Tucholsky with a citation from *Die Weltbühne*, 1930. The citation added plausibility but made it easy to show that the work was not from there. Nonetheless it was plausible enough that some German literature teachers had already included it in their curriculum according to Jakob Zirm [2008] in Die Presse. In fact, Zirm writes, it came from an Austrian named Richard Kerschhofer. Mere plausibility was enough to give the forgery some measure of success.

4.4 SOCIAL SCIENCES

4.4.1 INTRODUCTION

Several recent cases that reached the news show that data falsification is a significant problem in the social sciences. The Stapel case also involved giving manufactured data to ten doctoral students to use in their dissertations, which affected their lives [Budd, 2013]. Speculations about the causes often refer to the pressure on researchers to perform in order to get jobs, tenure, or promotion to higher levels, but this cannot be a complete answer. Budd et al. [2016] argues, for example, that "the pressure to publish and the gender of authors do not play a significant role..." Both James Hunton (U.S.) and Diederik Stapel (Netherlands) had permanent positions as full professor. That does not mean that they had no further ambitions or that the general pressure to show results did not affect them, but it does suggest that the reasons for their actions elude simple explanations. The reasons for their behavior could reasonably be a factor in the metrics for data falsification, in cases where the reasons followed a clear pattern. There may be a pattern, but it is unknown at this point and perhaps will not be known until the scholarly world has detected the full range of data falsification in the social sciences. Such cases need to be viewed with caution. The posthumous accusations that British psychologist Cyril Burt falsified his data seemed indisputable until Robert Joynson "came across an inconsistency in the case for the prosecution that had never really been followed through" [Blinkhorn, 1989]. The inconsistency was not proof, but did change minds, including that of Steven Blinkhorn, who discussed the Joynson [1989] book in *Nature*.

Detection is hard, as will be seen below in the discussion of both Stapel and Hunton. The ability to reproduce the data is the clearest and most cogent argument for genuineness. Unfortunately replication in the social sciences is both costly and chancy, because circumstances change. Replication studies are also discussed below.[5] One of the more troubling grayscale complications involving social science data results from updates to large-scale shared databases.[6] The intent of these updates is not falsification, but when the updates change historical data that earlier studies used, they also undermine the reliability of older studies and may invalidate their results.

One of the approaches to detecting data falsification uses a statistical analysis to assess whether a result set is too perfect or contains too little genuine randomness. These kinds of plausibility tests give more measurable results than the gut feelings of humanities and arts scholars, but interpretations of the results are equally vulnerable to scholarly desires to make new and exciting discoveries. A statistical outcome is a probability ratio, and everyone who has studied basic statistics known that $p < 0.05$ still means that 1 result in 20 could be different. Such an analysis needs to be part of a metric, but cannot be the single criterion. Equally important is the set of comparison data. If many datasets in a particular subject area show certain characteristics (including less randomness than in samples from other populations), that too needs to be taken into account.

Probably the most practical means of testing for data falsification at this point is to make the data fully accessible and to provide enough metadata to describe its origin, structure, and use. In effect, this uses crowdsourcing to test its validity. A crowdsourced analysis is not without its risks, though, especially in the social sciences where many people either misjudge their degree of technical expertise, or make convenient assumptions about the expertise of others. The result may both confirm bad data and lead to mistaken doubts about data that are in fact valid. With these caveats, however, exposing research data could help to expose falsification at the same time as it complies with governmental requirements for how to handle data from funded research.

4.4.2 REPLICATION STUDIES

Replication studies have become a significant theme in both economics and psychology in recent years, in part in response to data problems. Colin Camerer et al. [2016] recently looked at the results of a large set of replications in the article "Evaluating replicability of laboratory experiments in economics," and preface their article by saying:

> "The deepest trust in scientific knowledge comes from the ability to replicate empirical findings directly and independently. Although direct replication is widely applauded (1), it is rarely carried out in empirical social science. Replication is now more important than ever, because the quality of results has been questioned in many fields."

The results of some of the replications were disappointing and raised questions about the reliability of both data and conclusions:

---

[5]See Section 4.4.2, Replication Studies.
[6]See Section 4.4.5, Database Revisions.

"The recent Reproducibility Project: Psychology (RPP) replicated 100 original studies published in three top journals in psychology. The vast majority (97) of the original studies reported 'positive findings,' but in the replications, the RPP only found a significant effect in the same direction for 36% of these studies (19)." Footnote 19 leads to: "Open Science Collaboration, Science 349, aac4716 (2015)." [Camerer et al., 2016]

Any studies involving replicating experiments with humans can face the problem that perceptions and circumstances change over time in ways that potentially could subtly affect how participants behave, even when experimenters try to hold all factors steady.

The metrics for replication studies are somewhat complex. Counting the number of replications that find a significant effect in the same direction as the original study yields a 61% replication rate. But since there is "no universally agreed-upon standard," Camerer et al. use additional assessment methods, explained as follows:

"A complementary method for assessing replicability is to test whether the 95% confidence interval (CI) of the replication effect size includes the original effect size (19) [Cumming (21) discusses the interpretation of CIs for replications]. This is the case in 12 of our replications (66.7%). If we also include the study in which the entire 95% CI exceeds the original effect size, the number of replicable studies increases to 13 (72.2%). An alternative measure, which acknowledges sampling error in both the original study and the replications, is to count how many replicated effects lie in a 95% 'prediction interval' (24). This count is higher (83.3%) and increases to 88.9% if we also include the replication whose effect size exceeds the upper bound of the prediction interval (fig. S2 and supplementary materials, section 2)." [Camerer et al., 2016, p. 1434]

In the end an 83.3% replication result is good, not merely in comparison with the results from psychology, but also in comparison with general expectation, which was between 71.1% and 75.2% [Camerer et al., 2016]. This should not be taken as a reliable measure of the quality of research in psychology vs. economics, since the circumstances of the testing are generally different.

There is some reason to think that non-experimental data could provide better results, but if surveys and other human-based sources are included, that is not necessarily the case, as everyone knows who follows the ever changing results of political surveys. Camerer also reports results from some non-experimental studies:

"In economics, several studies have shown that statistical findings from nonexperimental data are not always easy to replicate (29). Two studies of macroeconomic findings, reported in the Journal of Money, Credit and Banking in 1986 and 2006, respectively found that only 13% and 23% of original results were replicable, even when the data and code were easily accessible (30, 31)." [Camerer et al., 2016, p. 1435]

Overall he sees a positive picture for the top economic journals, but limiting the study to top journals leaves questions open about the long tail of less rigorous and less competitive publications that publish a significant portion of the scholarly output. Nonetheless Camerer's suggestions make sense as a way to improve the reliability of replication in general:

> "Our study suggests that laboratory experiments published in top economic journals have relatively high rates of replicability. Challenges still remain: For example, executing replications can be laborious, even when scientific journals require online posting of data and computer code to make things easier. This is a reminder that as scientists, we should design and document our methods to anticipate replication and make it easy to do." [Camerer et al., 2016, p. 1436]

The idea that researchers should anticipate replication can apply to many fields. Posting the data allows scholars to work directly with the original data to test the analysis, and it exposes the data directly to plausibility tests that could expose falsification. Posting the "computer code" offers further transparency because it shows the core of the analysis.

This still leaves open potential issues about how the data were gathered and what they represent. For economic experiments, how the experiments were run is normally described in detail, but a detailed description is not quite the same as a full listing of all the nuances needed to replicate experiments, just as a detailed description of a computing system may not include the full range of environmental information necessary for installation at a new site on different hardware—as those with experience installing complex systems know well. A truly complete description may take on a certain narrative or even ethnographic character, and at a minimum the character of a lab notebook, where scientists record each step and each revision. Imperfect descriptions are too common to count as signs of falsification, but persons who falsify data may well manipulate descriptions of how they acquired the data to enhance plausibility, and those descriptions could offer a chance to develop metrics to help discover falsification.

4.4.3   DIEDERIK STAPEL

Diederik Stapel was a successful academic by the time he was in his mid 40s. He had a professorship, had served a term as dean, and had grant-funded research projects. At some point that is still unclear he stopped gathering data and began to manufacture it. Yudhidit Bhattacharjee [2013] wrote in his 2013 article "Diederik Stapel's Audacious Academic Fraud":

> "What the public didn't realize, he [Stapel] said, was that academic science, too, was becoming a business. 'There are scarce resources, you need grants, you need money, there is competition,' he said. 'Normal people go to the edge to get that money. Science is of course about discovery, about digging to discover the truth. But it is also communication, persuasion, marketing. I am a salesman. I am on the road. People are on the road with their talk. With the same talk. It's like a circus.'"

Stapel was a very successful salesman. He knew what editors and what grant reviewers wanted, and he could provide the kind of clear, clean, cogent prose that they looked for:

"In his early years of research—when he supposedly collected real experimental data— Stapel wrote papers laying out complicated and messy relationships between multiple variables. He soon realized that journal editors preferred simplicity. They are actually telling you: 'Leave out this stuff. Make it simpler,' Stapel told me. Before long, he was striving to write elegant articles." [Bhattacharjee, 2013]

The explanation that editors wanted simplicity and elegance likely has an element of truth, but was also self-serving in shifting responsibility. He had enough experience with real data to be able to create a very plausible fictional account of the data gathering with situations and stories so plausible that there was no incentive to investigate too closely. Just as art forgers would paint pictures that experts imagined should have existed, Stapel fabricated data that his audience was predisposed to believe. Details mattered. Here is his description of one fabricated situation:

"To get a behavioral measure of discrimination related to stereotyping, travelers were asked to fill out the short questionnaire in an area where there were six chairs lined up. Respondents (who were all Caucasians) could choose any chair, except that the first chair in the row was already taken by either a black (Dutch-African) or white (Dutch-Caucasian) confederate. Through random assignment, for half of the participants this confederate was a 20-year-old male Dutch-African (black) person, and for the other half, the confederate was a (20-year-old) male Dutch-Caucasian (white) person. Pretests had shown that these two confederates were judged as equally intelligent, friendly, attractive, and approachable. The dependent variable was the distance in number of chairs (zero to four) between the chair with the confederate and the chair the participant chose to sit on." [Stapel and Lindenberg, 2011]

The description sounds convincing, but when Stapel returned to the station in Utrecht where the experiment supposedly took place, he could not find the location.

"On his return trip to Tilburg, Stapel stopped at the train station in Utrecht. This was the site of his study linking racism to environmental untidiness, supposedly conducted during a strike by sanitation workers. … Now, looking around during rush hour, as people streamed on and off the platforms, Stapel could not find a location that matched the conditions described in his experiment." [Bhattacharjee, 2013]

The chief detail that mattered here was the set of six chairs. He might have argued that the chair configuration had changed since his experiment, but further investigation with the railroad authorities could have confirmed or denied that. Originally he could have picked a specific real location (with chairs in the right configuration), or have adapted his story to another plausible set of chairs, but apparently he did not take the trouble.

In another experiment in the same paper, Stapel described the situation in even more detail:

"In the second field experiment, we tried to address this issue by manipulating environmental disorder while keeping cleanness constant (17). ... Disorder was manipulated by some subtle environmental interventions. We took out and misplaced some of the tiles in the pavement of the sidewalk, put a badly parked car (with two wheels on the sidewalk, windows open) near the spot w[h]ere respondents were interviewed, and put a bicycle on the street, as if it had been abandoned. ... In the control condition (that was run a day later), the same pavement, car, and bicycle were there, but everything looked nice and neat." [Stapel and Lindenberg, 2011]

The details sound very plausible, but recognizing the exact street could be a problem, and there was a risk that people in the neighborhood might have noticed, though of course he could have explained away their not remembering after some years.

Discovering research fraud is as hard as unmasking forgery. The issue that troubles many scholars, editors, and publishers is how much undiscovered fraud remains, and there are no good tools to use for testing. Martin Enserink [2012] writes about "an unpublished statistical method to detect data fraud" in his article "Fraud-Detection Tool Could Shake Up Psychology" in the journal *Science*. He goes on to say:

"The technique was developed by Uri Simonsohn, a social psychologist at the Wharton School of the University of Pennsylvania, who tells Science that he has also notified a U.S. university of a psychology paper his method flagged. That paper's main author, too, has been investigated and has resigned, he says. As Science went to press, Simonsohn said he planned to reveal details about his method, and both cases, as early as this week."

Simonsohn [2014] published his article "Just post it: the lesson from two cases of fabricated data detected by statistics alone" in *Psychological Science* in 2013. He begins by advocating posting the data publicaly so that others can analyze it. He goes on to say:

"In this article, I illustrate how raw data can be analyzed for identifying likely fraud through two case studies. Each began with the observation that summary statistics reported in a published article were too similar across conditions to have originated in random samples, an approach to identifying problematic data that has been employed before..."

In the first case, he writes: "Although means differed dramatically across conditions, the standard deviations were almost identical" (p. 1877). He went on to investigate how likely the coincidence was. The second case was about an unusual similarity of means. The authors admitted a possible coding error and offered a story about how participants may have coded the answers as they did, but "neither [explanation] could account for the excessive similarity of means or the evenness of scores across conditions. If anything, these features of the data-generating process would cause the opposite pattern: more rather than less variation" [Simonsohn, 2014, p. 1882].

What Simonsohn offers is not a tool like iThenticate, but an approach to thinking about the plausibility of the statistical results. This approach has the virtue of clear metrics that an editor or a commission could use to draw conclusions, but it still relies on a probability analysis and does not completely rule out the possibility of a statistically unlikely event. Simonsohn took the following measures to avoid making false accusations:

> "First, replicate analyses across multiple studies before suspecting foul play by a given author. Second, compare suspected studies with similar ones by other authors. Third, extend analyses to raw data. Fourth, contact authors privately and transparently, and give them ample time to consider your concerns. Fifth, offer to discuss matters with a trusted statistically savvy advisor. Sixth, give the authors more time. Finally, if suspicions remain, convey them only to entities tasked with investigating such matters, and do so as discreetly as possible." [Simonsohn, 2014, p. 1886]

These are sensible measures, but plainly time-consuming on a large scale, and still leaves people to rely on a plausibility analysis to make an initial decision about whether to investigate further. An author who avoids certain obvious mistakes could still falsify data without detection.

4.4.4   JAMES HUNTON

The case of James Hunton received less public attention than Diederik Stapel. There is no *New York Times* story, and only one in the *Boston Globe* announcing Hunton's resignation [Healy, 2012]. Hunton was a well-known accounting researcher. According to the "Report of Judith A. Malone, Bentley University Ethics Officer, concerning Dr. James E. Hunton" [Malone, 2014], Hunton had "published approximately 50 papers while at Bentley, and there is reason to believe that many of those papers involved data that were provided by Dr. Hunton alone..."

Suspicion arose first in a paper that Hunton wrote together with Anna Gold of Erasmus University, Rotterdam, "A Field Experiment Comparing the Outcomes of Three Fraud Brainstorming Procedures: Nominal Group, Round Robin, and Open Discussion." The paper included a simple reporting error:

> "In a nutshell, the company misrepresented the number of U.S.-based offices it had: not 150, as the paper maintained (and as a reader had noticed might be on the high side, triggering an inquiry from the journal), but quite a bit less than that. In fact, the 150 figure came from combining U.S. offices with international outposts …an important difference, to be sure, but not one that necessarily would kill the paper." ["amarcus41", 2012]

As Retraction Watch noted, a simple misstatement that did not materially affect the outcome of the paper would not normally merit a retraction, but only a correction. Nonetheless suspicion went further. The retraction notice states:

"The authors confirmed a misstatement in the article and were unable to provide supporting information requested by the editor and publisher. Accordingly, the article has been retracted." [Hunton and Gold, 2012]

The absence of "supporting information" became more of a problem as questions arose. A second retraction came from *Contemporary Accounting Research*, and the more the Bentley investigators raised questions, the more doubts grew. Malone wrote:

"In both the case of Fraud Brainstorming and Tone at the Top, Dr. Hunton was the only author who had any access to the original data or to the identity of the firms that were supposedly the sources of the data. Dr. Hunton repeatedly told Bentley, his co-authors and journal editors that strict confidentiality agreements prevented him from sharing with them the original data or the identities of the CPA firm (the supposed source of the data reported in Fraud Brainstorming) and the consulting/training firm (the supposed source of the data reported in Tone at the Top). He claimed that disclosure of either the data or the identities of the firms would result in him being subject to lawsuits, to the loss of his CPA license, and to a loss of confidence in the field and thus access to further research opportunities." [Malone, 2014]

Hunton could not, however, provide convincing versions of the confidentiality agreements. As Malone continued following up details, the evidence of fraud grew:

"One of the firms, whose name appeared in one version of a confidentiality agreement, reviewed the document at Bentley's request and reported that it bore no resemblance to any document that it ever used with research partners." [Malone, 2014]

When Bentley used a digital forensics firm to analyze Hunton's hard drive, they found "that his laptop had been wiped clean of all of his electronic files" [Malone, 2014]. It was clear that Hunton had tried to eliminate evidence of fraud:

"The consultant's forensic analysis and recovery efforts revealed that Dr. Hunton's laptop once housed a great deal of electronic data, and revealed no evidence to suggest that the data had been inadvertently lost. To the contrary, the forensic analysis discovered that an 'eraser' utility had been loaded onto the laptop during the fall of 2012. This analysis also revealed that a second utility, which permits users to manipulate the creation dates in certain metadata fields in certain kinds of files, had also been loaded onto the laptop during the fall of 2012. Further analysis determined that the eraser utility had been run multiple times during that fall in an attempt (only partially successful) to delete all of the files on the laptop—including the metadata manipulation utility." [Malone, 2014]

As with Stapel's case, Hunton made small mistakes in the details about how he presented his research. It seems likely that other suspicions played a role as well, perhaps a concern that the statistics had implausible anomalies, such as Simonsohn used in his testing. Statistics are sufficiently complicated, however, that detecting falsification requires a level of expertise that goes well beyond introductory courses. The fact is that odd results and uncommon regularities can and do occur in isolated cases, and without the original data, actual proof that the results are not coincidence can remain elusive.

Hunton only provided summary results. If he had taken the trouble to create a full set of data, and had taken time to create plausible confidentiality agreements, he may have escaped being caught. Forging plausible physical evidence such as a confidentiality agreement is harder, because it involves company formats and names of people whom investigators could ask. It is theoretically possible, however. Persons who want systematically to commit fraud could learn how to avoid mistakes from public cases like this—assuming, of course, that they are willing to take the time to create all the necessary details and to make them consistent.

The effort involved in data forgery is one of the factors that helps with detection. With the forgery of art works or the forgery of documents, the effort has a clear monetary reward. Forging data to get yet another scholarly publication has only indirect financial and social incentives: a better job, better salary, more respect. One of the strongest forces that helps detection is the human tendency toward satisficing, that is, toward doing the least necessary to accomplish a goal. Both Stapel and Hunton could have created better forgeries, if they tried harder.

4.4.5   DATABASE REVISIONS

Shared databases are increasingly important in social science research, and researchers generally assume that the data are safe from any form of manipulation. These databases can be especially important for replication studies on the assumption that they provide a stable and consistent source. A recent paper in the Social Science Research Network (SSRN) suggests that this may not be true for the I/B/E/S data that are available through the Wharton Research Data Services and are widely used by both financial analysts and economics and business researchers in universities. In the paper "Changes in the I/B/E/S Database and their Effect on the Observed Properties of Analyst Forecasts," by Andrew Call, May Hewitt, Jessica Watkins and Teri Lombardi Yohn (posted to SSRN 03 June, 2016), the authors write:

"A comparison of these two files reveals a net decrease in the number of individual earnings forecasts, unique firms covered, unique forecasting analysts, and unique brokerages from the OLD to the NEW file during our sample period, suggesting a loss of information about analyst earnings forecasts due to changes to the historical record on I/B/E/S. Specifically, 12 percent of analyst earnings forecasts reported in the OLD file are not available in the NEW file. Further, about 6 percent of the observations in the NEW file did not exist in the OLD file, and another 9 percent of the forecasts exist in both files (i.e., same firm, same analyst, same forecast date) but with a different forecasted value across the two files. Overall, these adjustments to the database represent more than 26 percent of the OLD file. We also find that the changes we document are more prevalent in the latter years of our sample. Specifically, the percentage of changes to the OLD (NEW) file almost doubles from approximately 13 percent (11 percent) for forecasts made in 1993 to approximately 25 percent (20 percent) of forecasts made in 2006, the last full year in our sample." [Call et al., 2016, p. 2]

In effect this means that the firms that supply the data have quietly been changing the historical record without making those changes clear in the descriptions about the data. It means that any attempt to replicate an analysis made years earlier would come out differently, if the historical data from the current database were used. Such changes could be justified if the changes corrected past errors, and that is partly true, but introduces a bias:

"We find that the analyst forecast properties vary considerably across the OLD and NEW files. The earnings forecasts in the NEW file are significantly more accurate than the earnings forecasts in the OLD file. Further, the earnings forecasts are significantly less biased and more bold in the NEW file than in the OLD file. Therefore, one would obtain a more favorable impression of the properties of analyst earnings forecasts with the NEW file than with the OLD file." [Call et al., 2016, p. 2]

In other words, one of the reasons for the change is to make the analysts' forecasts look better. This paper is too new to have generated much reaction, and it is still in draft form, which means revisions will likely come. Nonetheless the evidence that the data were manipulated will likely have consequences for researchers who use this database.

4.4.6   DATA MANIPULATION

Data falsification can affect genuine data that researchers have manipulated in order to get a particular result. In general the disciplines have rules of thumb for how much and what kind of manipulation is allowed. Editors and readers can calculate the metrics themselves if the original data are made available along with the final set. Some reasonable guesses are also possible if an author describes the manipulations in sufficient detail to give a clear idea about what changes took place.

Outliers and careless responses in survey data are a good example. Oppenheimer et al. (2009) argue that satisficing often plays a role, in the article "Instructional manipulation checks: Detecting satisficing to increase statistical power," in the *Journal of Experimental Social Psychology*:

"Krosnick noted that responding to surveys often requires a great deal of cognitive effort (Krosnick, 1991; Krosnick, Narayan, & Smith, 1996). He hypothesized that participants might satisfice by choosing the first (as opposed to best) alternative that fits the question or, in extreme cases, by answering randomly." [Oppenheimer et al., 2009]

A person who seemingly answered the survey questions randomly creates data that can reasonably be removed from the sample, but choosing the first alternative that fits (instead of the best) is harder to discover. A tool to show that satisficing took place (which Oppenheimer et al. propose) can justify correcting data by throwing out unreliable answers.

Especially difficult are questions that involve some degree of error on the part of the survey writers. A survey that the author of this monograph helped to design some years ago asked students in Germany to mark whether they had a bachelor's or master's degree or a "Diplom," which is treated variously as a bachelor's or master's degree. Many students marked the "other" category, and from the answers it became plain that they had marked "other" because the old German "Magister" was not in the list, and the respondents did not equate it with the more contemporary master's degree, even though that now is commonly done. This confusion meant that the number of responses for master's degrees was too low, and that people with the "Magister" inflated the other category. It was possible to develop an algorithm for adjusting the answers, but the algorithm was clearly a manipulation that required sophisticated justification.

Survey researchers often use models, and Nate Silver's Fivethirtyeight blog has the virtue of giving clear explanations of his models. In his case, he is not throwing out outliers or attempting to adjust flawed answers, but explicitly adding external data or correction factors to get an outcome that he believes more nearly reflects reality than the original data:

"Differences between polls-plus and polls only

- Polls-plus combines polls with an economic index; polls-only does not.
- Polls-plus will include a convention bounce adjustment; polls-only will not.
- Polls-plus starts by assuming that likely voter polls are better for Republicans; polls-only makes no such assumption. Both models revise this assumption as more data becomes available.
- Polls-plus subtracts points from third-party candidates early in the race, while polls-only does not …" [Silver, 2016].

The legitimacy test for Nate Silver's analysis is his ability to predict the outcome of elections, and as he writes: "It's mostly the same model as the one we used to successfully forecast the 2008 and 2012 elections" [Silver, 2016].

4.5   NATURAL SCIENCES

4.5.1   INTRODUCTION

The natural sciences are diverse, and that diversity means that there are no simple metrics for data falsification. This work will divide the natural sciences into four broad groups: the lab sciences (where data originate largely from group work), the medical sciences (where the data come from complex human reactions), computing and statistics (where the data generally come from external sources), and the non-lab sciences (where data collection may be more individual). As a rule, the natural sciences deal with relatively large amounts of data and often relatively public amounts of data in fields where there happens to be a culture of sharing, such as astronomy.

Natural science data often lack transparency simply because the meanings are not easily translated into natural language. A set of measurements from a machine or from laboratory tests may consist of numerical values that make sense only to those with training in a specific field. A common medical example comes from blood tests, where the meaning of amounts of and relationships between high-density lipoprotein (HDL) and low-density lipoprotein (LDL)—the so-called good and bad types of cholesterol—has changed over time. Even genuine data can be difficult to interpret and lead to false conclusions, which can make the discovery of false data harder because the purpose of the falsification may be obscure.

As with the Stapel and Hunton cases above, creating plausible fake data involves considerable domain knowledge in order to have the data look at all real to a well-informed reviewer. Amateur fakes can often be discovered quickly. Others cannot, as Furman et al. [2012] reported in "Governing knowledge in the scientific community: Exploring the role of retractions in biomedicine":

> "In 2006, news that high-profile scientific papers describing the creation of human embryonic stem cells from cloning and somatic cell nuclear transfer were fraudulent roiled the academic community (Kennedy, 2006). In 2002, Bell Labs scientist Jan Hendrik Schön (rumored to have been a candidate for the Nobel Prize) was found to have falsified analysis in numerous publications, including in papers in top journals Science and Nature, over a four-year period (Reich, 2009). In 2009, Scott S. Reuben, a physician-scientist funded by Pfizer for research on analgesia, confessed to having fabricated data in more than 20 papers (Kowalczyk, 2009)." [Furman et al., 2012]

The Hendrik Schön case offers some insight into how the fabrication was done. Eugenie Samuel Reich (2009) writes in the article "The rise and fall of a physics fraudster":

> "Three years later, in 2002, Schön revealed to his investigators how he had actually done it. He was doing science backward. He started from the conclusion he wanted and then assembled data to show it. Although Schön did have several wired-up pentacene crystals in the lab in Murray Hill and in Konstanz, his own writing suggests that he was taking his inspiration rather more from his understanding of other scientists' expectations. Having created a field-effect transistor set-up that was understood by colleagues to work well, Schön began to claim further advances, always following predictions and expectations. When one colleague suggested that he might be able to tune the crystals into a superconducting state, Schön agreed, and produced the data." [Reich, 2009]

Manufacturing the data gave him the opportunity to make them look exactly like high-quality results:

> "His resistance curves did not look at all like the kind of data that might have arisen from a sloppy experiment. They had a larger-than-life, doubt-dispelling, quality.

Schön knew this, because he later told investigators that he had used an equation to calculate a very smooth sweep of data, in order to avoid doubt. When scientists doubt others' claims, they tend to ask detailed questions about the method that has produced them—questions that Schön must have known he would have struggled to answer. The smooth data helped to stall inquiries." [Reich, 2009]

The fact that Schön knew the questions people would ask and adjusted his data to avoid them was a trick only a person with excellent domain knowledge could have. The metrics that could have helped detection included the unlikelihood of his "very smooth sweep of data," but too much skepticism toward good results can also seem like jealousy and makes people reluctant to push the issue. In the end hubris is often the weakness of people creating fraudulent data in the natural sciences. A single set of fake data might go unnoticed and if noticed, might be attributed to error. Repetition increases the likelihood of exposure.

4.5.2   LAB SCIENCES

Fraud is ordinarily a solitary business and the collective nature of research in the lab sciences tends to allow fewer opportunities for an individual to fabricate or falsify data. This may be the reason that instances of pure data fabrication in the lab sciences are relatively rare compared to the wealth of publication. A conspiracy to create fraudulent data is almost unheard of and would run considerable risk of whistleblowing in all except perhaps the most hierarchical societies. Even on occasions where a single lab member handles a particular aspect of an experiment, output from a machine or a separate chemical test, the likelihood of someone noticing actual falsification is non-trivial.

Another fact of life in the lab sciences is replication. Not every scientific result becomes a building block for future study, but unusual and noteworthy results often do, and it is precisely those kind of results that people tend to fake. Unfortunately exposing the data to replication does not solve the whole of the problem, as Maiväli writes in "Chapter 1–Do We Need a Science of Science?":

"Stroebe et al. analyzed the output of 36 notorious scientific cheats (caught between 1974 and 2012), who had published a total of 804 certifiably fraudulent papers. ... Of those frauds only two were discovered because of a failure to replicate findings. One of the two involved a 1982 failed self-replication of his results by an ex-postdoc, asked for by his suspicious coauthors." [Maiväli, 2015]

In this case "self-replication" sounds less like deliberate fraud than a mistake, though of course the co-authors may have been watching more closely the second time. What seems more important here is the suspicion on the part of the co-authors. Co-authors played no role in the Hunton case and the doctoral students who raised questions about Stapel were academic dependents rather than co-authors. The nature of co-authorship is different in a large lab group than among a small set of professors who generally share social ties as well as professional interests.

A lab group may of course also have close internal social ties, but larger lab groups often function more like a small business, where blind trust is less commonly the rule than cross-checking. Maiväli continues:

> "The other involved a fraudster, who must have been really desperate as he chose to 'discover' a new element for the periodic table (element 118). In the new element discovery business the rule is that another group must reproduce any discovery, before it can be accepted. In the event three groups tried and failed." [Maiväli, 2015]

This sounds less like deliberate fraud than sloppy work. An environment where replication is normal seems likely to discourage pure fabrication, which could itself explain why replication exposed so few cases.

4.5.3 MEDICAL SCIENCES

The medical sciences are rife with retractions. The Retraction Watch category "clinical studies" has 1,057 retractions. Data falsification appears to play a role in less than 10%, perhaps because of how the data are classified. The U.S. Office of Research Integrity, which deals only with cases involving public health research, lists 46 "cases in which administrative actions were imposed due to findings of research misconduct" [Office of Research Integrity, 2016]. All appear to involve some form of fabricated data, many of which seem to involve image manipulation (which will be discussed in the next chapter). Discovering falsified data in the medical sciences is hard in part because the data themselves are complex, and falsifying results by manipulating imperfect data is certainly easier and more plausible than attempting to invent completely fraudulent results. Manipulation will be discussed more in the section on computing and statistics, since they are typically some of the tools involved.[7]

One noted lab science case involved the Korean researcher Hwang Woo Suk, whose stem cell research won enough attention to give him hero status in Korea. He claimed to be able to clone dogs, and to have created human embryonic stem stells. Péter Kalkuk explains in his article "The Legacy of the Hwang Case: Research Misconduct in Biosciences":

> "This new technological advance would provide a method to create biological materials that are immunologically and genetically matched to patients." [Kakuk, 2009]

The aura of success began to crumble when a U.S. collaborator, Gerald Schatten, asked to have his name removed from a paper for ethical reasons involving the egg donations. The ethical concerns led to a broader-scale investigation:

> "The SNU [Seoul National University] report discusses the method and the process of fabrication in detail, furthermore it establishes that all the data of the 2005 publication was fabricated, including: results of tests from DNA fingerprinting, photographs of

---

[7]See Section 4.5.4, Computing and Statistics.

teratoma, embryoid bodies, MHC-HLA isotype matches and karyotyping. Regarding the 2004 paper, 23 samples were examined for DNA fingerprinting analysis by three independent centers, and all of these obtained identical results that brought forth the conclusion of the panel: 'results described in 2004 Science article including DNA fingerprinting analyses and photographs of cells have also been fabricated.' " [Kakuk, 2009]

Apparently some of the false data came from a "digital manipulation of the pictures" [Kakuk, 2009], but the full extent of data falsification remained unclear:

"Hwang apologized for the fiasco at a press conference, but he denied deceit. In this talk at Seoul's National Press Center on the 12th January he accused the other members of the research team of deceiving him with false data, he referred to conspiracy, sabotage and the possibility of theft of materials from the laboratory." [Kakuk, 2009]

Korea is somewhat of a special case because of the strong hierarchical loyalties. The interesting fact in terms of metrics for falsification is that no one appears to have examined the data proving Hwang's claims until the ethical scandal broke. It seems plausible that replication would have failed, but the techniques seemed daunting enough that no one seems to have tried.

J. Hein et al (2012) in the paper "Scientific fraud in 20 falsified anesthesia papers" in the Journal *Der Anaesthesist* has a recommendation for discovering false data in medical research by using a technique from financial auditing that involves number patterns: "Data from natural sources show counter-intuitive distribution patterns for the leading digits to the left of the decimal point and the digit 1 is observed more frequently than all other numbers." The authors go on to explain:

"In 2009 a total of 21 papers which the author admitted were fictitious ... were retracted from several anesthesia and other scientific journals. The present study investigates for the first time, whether these studies can be detected as false using the method described by Benford and Newcomb." [Hein et al., 2012]

This paper has had no great impact (4 citations according to the Web of Science, and 8 according to Google Scholar). There is no evidence that the method has been used for fraud detection among the medical or even anaesthesiological journals, but it does represent an approach that could provide some metrics using a probability calculation.

4.5.4 COMPUTING AND STATISTICS

Computing and statistics are not fields that generally produce their own data, but are used to analyze data in other disciplines. This fits with the Retraction Watch statistics where the 38 articles listed under computer science had plagiarism, ethics, and other forms of problems, but not data fraud. The same is true for statistics, which has only 10 retractions listed, mainly for errors in statistical tests. This section will look at how computing and statistics can be used to manipulate and falsify data from other sources. It will also look at how computing and statistical tools can be used to fabricate data—a task that was at one time a standard part of computer science training in order to create data to test new programs.

Computing

Computer programs represent a standard tool for almost all of the natural and many of the social sciences. Their importance is growing even in the humanities as text mining and "distant reading" (as Franco Moretti calls it) take off in importance. In very broad terms, programs are used for: (1) selection, (2) manipulation, and (3) analysis.

Selection means writing a program that will go through a mass of data to cull out relevant items. Data sets and databases often have heterogeneous content, much of which is not relevant for a particular study. A bibliometric study using the Web of Science database may, for example, want only to look at citations in articles about "cliometrics," which is broadly a statistical analysis of historical economic data. A simple search on the Web of Science gives 162,286 results and includes a wide range of topics including some in business economics that may not be relevant to an analysis of cliometrics. A researcher may well want to set a more precise definition that excludes articles that look at more recent economic analyses and focuses perhaps on pre-1900 content. This kind of selection and limitation is entirely legitimate, but could be considered falsification if the researcher has already done enough analysis to know that the results will be different if the search used a different boundary, and the boundary choice is made primarily to force the desired results, not on more valid scholarly grounds. Selection has many possible subtleties that require an understanding of the data, the meaning of the fields, and the likelihood of error. Honest errors are easy to commit in cases where the data contain irregularities that may be as minor as the difference between a comma and a semicolon in an author sequence, or the use of a comma instead of a decimal point in a numeric sequence.[8] Detecting coding errors is part of any selection process, and it involves a measure of judgment about whether to change or alter data points that are presumed to be wrong. Often there is no clear right or wrong in the selection process. An unscrupulous researcher can make plausible-sounding choices that shift results in a particular direction. A comparison, as in plagiarism cases, is a reasonable if rarely practiced approach. Comparing two data sets to discover differences is a relatively simple computing exercise.

Metrics could be used to compare an original data set with the one used for analysis, if the original data and the set used for analysis were both available. A careful researcher might do this as part of the write-up, and a space-conscious editor may delete such a write-up to keep the page count down (even with digital publication, many journals still have page count limits). A scholar told me recently about an online journal requiring her to delete the code book from an article, because of word count and page count limits. The problem has not vanished in the digital world.

---

[8]A comma is the standard separator in German between the integer and decimal part of a number—and decimals are used in numbers where English speakers use commas—which makes errors easy when switching languages.

Data sometimes require a certain amount of clean-up that involves legitimate manipulation. An example comes from a paper the author of this monograph wrote some years ago, where there was a question whether to match on the ISSN (International Standard Serial Number) or on the title. I decided in favor of the title on the theory that the people entering the ISSN were more likely to enter the digits wrong, but then had to check cases where two titles were similar enough that data entry errors could account for the difference, and had to adjust the names. A manipulation of this sort leaves room for bias, depending on whether the researcher wants to find more or fewer matches. Later I discovered that the ISSN number came directly from the publisher, which used ISSN as the key field and tolerated some title variants. This meant that an ISSN match would have been more reliable and using even a cleaned-up name field may have reduced the match-count. Since the paper wanted to show significant overlap, the choice turned out to be a conservative one that probably underrepresented the desired result, but it could have been the other way around.

Plagiarism checkers do not manipulate the data they examine, but they make choices about how much stemming[9] to employ and how many words in a sequence count as a match. It is also possible with some checking systems to choose longer or shorter matches, and turning stemming on and off could also have a marked effect on the result. This kind of choice does not actually change the data, but similar choices can change the file by creating a working file that counts more than the "raw" data set.

Errors often occur in the analysis portion of a program. They can be completely innocent, such as adding the wrong number because the variable names are so similar that they are easily confused. A deliberate falsification of results is also possible and can be disguised with different techniques. One technique is to write in a language that relatively few people know and to provide few or misleading comments so that any (deliberate) error could be excused as a mistake. Assembly language works well for this, since assembly language programming has become a rare skill, and the commenting is notoriously bad. A variant that would disguise falsification even better is to modify the actual machine code of the executable version of a program. Some new techniques for making more efficient use of multi-core chips involve going into the executable code to reprogram loops to export the processing simultaneously to other cores in the chip. This is not for amateur programmers, but can be done. If a replication study wanted the code, there is no reason why they would necessarily recompile (and reassemble) the source code, and if they did, a programmer could give plausible technical reasons for the variation in results on different hardware.

Less sophisticated programmers can use other obfuscation techniques. In a language like Python that is relatively easy to read, even for those with little programming experience, it easy to set up an embedded series of functions (routines) that make it easy for a casual reader to fail to see a sequence of commands that could affect the data and change the analysis. The trigger for such functions could be data points that weaken or change the desired result and would not affect other data. One metric for this kind of falsification is the depth of the function sequences.

---

[9]"Stemming" is the process of reducing inflected words to their root or "stem."

Another is the degree to which the function names clearly express their purpose. This is not to suggest that multiple layers of function sequences are necessarily bad or that all unclear names imply an attempt to deceive, but they can be indications that suspicion could be warranted.

Statistics

Like computing, statistics are a standard tool for most of the sciences and social sciences, and like computing, many who use statistics as a tool have a limited expertise in a few aspects that are relevant to their research area. Some users are not completely sure about the reliability of tests under conditions where the data tend to deviate from what the test expects, and may inadvertently use the wrong test. Such errors are not evidence of deliberate falsification, but a repeated series of such errors can awaken suspicions. Statistics has rules about how tests should be carried out, including various (sometimes conflicting) recommendations about when to eliminate outliers. Outliers are complicated because they represent exceptions. The U.S. government NIST (National Institute of Standards and Technologies) *Engineering Statistics Handbook* online (2013) gives the following definition of outliers:

> "An outlier is an observation that lies an abnormal distance from other values in a random sample from a population. In a sense, this definition leaves it up to the analyst (or a consensus process) to decide what will be considered abnormal. Before abnormal observations can be singled out, it is necessary to characterize normal observations." [NIST, 2013]

The Handbook suggests a method to determine outliers by using a box plot to divide the data into quartiles and to calculate the interquartile range: "If the lower quartile is Q1 and the upper quartile is Q3, then the difference (Q3 - Q1) is called the interquartile range or IQ" [NIST, 2013].

> "The following quantities (called fences) are needed for identifying extreme values in the tails of the distribution:
>
> 1. lower inner fence: Q1 - 1.5*IQ
> 2. upper inner fence: Q3 + 1.5*IQ
> 3. lower outer fence: Q1 - 3*IQ
> 4. upper outer fence: Q3 + 3*IQ
>
> A point beyond an inner fence on either side is considered a mild outlier. A point beyond an outer fence is considered an extreme outlier." [NIST, 2013]

It is important to recognize two issues here. One is the relatively clear set of fences for mild and extreme outliers, and the other is the clear statement that in the end it is "up to the analyst (or a consensus process)" to make a final decision. The reasons for throwing out outliers matter, and those reasons depend on specific local and disciplinary circumstances. In the end, the agreement must convince others. The fences provide key metrics to aid the decision, but circumstances can exist where a mild outlier could be discarded and an extreme one kept.

The case of Ulrich Lichtenthaler illustrates one set of problems with statistics. He was a professor at the business school at the Otto Beisheim School of Management at WHU (Wissenschaftliche Hochschule für Unternehmungsführung) who not only duplicated papers, but who, according to Ivan Oransky [2012] in his Retraction Watch article, admitted that "that the statistical significance of several of the findings had been misreported or exaggerated."

In the same Retraction Watch article journal editor Russ Coff was quoted as saying:

> "Further investigation confirmed specific irregularities as well as a broader pattern. For example, in some cases where the coefficients and standard errors are about the same size, variables are reported as highly significant, This problem is more evident for independent variables than control variables." [Oransky, 2012]

As the number of his retracted papers grew, Lichtenthaler's co-author, Holger Ernst, also came under scrutiny. Alison McCook quotes the University's report in her article "German dept head reprimanded for not catching mistakes of co-author Lichtenthaler" in Retraction Watch:

> "The committee does, however, find fault with Professor Ernst as a co-author with Dr. Lichtenthaler, [for] having not sufficiently reviewed his work for mistakes, and the commission judges this behavior as severe scientific misconduct." [McCook, 2015]

The essence of the argument against Ernst is that that statistical errors were evident enough that he should have discovered them on his own. The fact is, however, that co-authors tend not to check each other's work. Effective co-authorship depends to a significant degree on trust, which increasingly has a risk attached to it.

4.5.5   OTHER NON-LAB SCIENCES

Another example from the non-lab science comes from Marc Hauser, a former Harvard professor, who was accused of misconduct. According to Carolyn Johnson, writing for the *Boston Globe*, the Harvard report said:

> "We did not find evidence that [Professor] Hauser has been inventing findings out of whole cloth," the committee wrote. " ... Hauser's shortcomings in respect to research integrity have in the main consisted instead of repeated instances of cutting corners, of pushing analyses of data further in the direction of significance than the actual findings warranted, and of reporting results as he may have wished them to have been, rather than as they actually were." [Johnson, 2014]

Hauser struggled against the findings, even suggesting that "someone had doctored a videotape of raw data showing monkeys responding to sounds," but no evidence of this was found [Johnson, 2014]. Instead there was evidence that he changed the data:

"The committee painstakingly reconstructed the process of data analysis and determined that Hauser had changed values, causing the result to be statistically significant, an important criterion showing that findings are probably not due to chance. For example, after the data from one experiment were analyzed in 2005, the results initially were not statistically significant. After Hauser informed a member of his lab of this by e-mail, he wrote a second e-mail: 'Hold the horses. I think I [expletive] something up on the coding. Let me get back to you.' After correcting for that problem, he concluded that the result was statistically significant. According to the Harvard report, five data points had changed from the original file, and four of the five changes were in the direction of making the result statistically significant." [Johnson, 2014]

When researchers believe that their ideas are right and feel frustrated that the evidence is imperfect, the temptation to alter the data to conform to their beliefs is very human, but violates basic premises of scientific integrity. The risk he took in altering the data was a form of arrogance based on the assumption that no one would check. The fact that others began checking his results and trying to replicate experiments should have served as a warning.

4.6   CONCLUSION

Data falsification and fabrication take many forms, far more than plagiarism, which enables direct comparisons between putative copying and original sources. That makes integrity problems with data harder to detect and to measure, because there is no single metric that works for the whole variety of possible falsification and fabrication. Nonetheless, a few important themes emerge from the case studies discussed in this chapter.

Many of the cases involved data fabrication, which should be the easiest data problem to discover because the barriers to doing it right are high. As a general rule fabricated data in the humanities has to do with physical media, such as paintings or supposedly original texts. The ability to get around physical tests on wood, canvas, paint, paper, and ink requires a certain knowledge of chemistry and where to get enough original materials to create a work that will not fail the first battery of tests. This would be a very high barrier, if the physical tests were a matter of routine. In fact, rare works are bought and sold all the time without much testing. Plausibility is the test that most people rely on, especially experts, who have reason to think their judgment is good, since it ordinarily is, and the fact is that physical tests cost money and take time. Unless there is suspicion, the incentive is not to use them. Provenance plays a role in establishing plausibility, and evidence of provenance can be faked.

Metrics for plausibility are certainly possible to establish. Often plausibility judgments are treated as black and white, even when the language tends to imply a gray scale when people say that something "looks" real or has the "hallmarks" of a genuine work. Very few scholarly experts will make the flat statement "this is genuine." They cite reasons, elements of evidence, circumstances that make the case plausible. The degree of hesitation and the amount of qualification in making a statement is measurable. Scholars who were asked to indicate their judgment on a Likert scale likely would not pick an extreme, especially in complex cases. Those over-interpreting expert opinions as certainties bear some fault for false judgments. Accepting a cautious statement as if it were certain flatters the person making it by implying that the person's core judgment is so sound that doubts do not matter, and few people are fully flattery-resistant.

Data falsification is even harder to detect because the changes are often small, perhaps only a few data points in a larger sample. The effort to check each data set for a plausible distribution is a barrier to discovery. Without some reason for suspicion, the cost of checking is not worth the trouble, and asking to check the work of a senior colleague or an old friend can lead to socially awkward situations. Access to the original data can be a problem in checking. The original data may no longer exist or require extra clean-up. It is remarkably easy to falsify data in ways that are hard to check later, especially if a person thinks through the likely questions in advance. Those who are caught often make mistakes: data that are overly perfect, or a source that can be exposed as untrue, or data that show a pattern so remarkable that others will want to test whether they can disprove it.

In theory peer review ought to catch data falsification problems, but few peer reviewers invest the time to examine the data in detail, or the data are not available to them. More often they look at the analysis and make judgments about how plausible the analysis seems and how logical the presentation is. Peer review is only occasionally remunerated. More often it is regarded as a public service that scholars undertake as a social obligation, and under the pressure of other deadlines, it is not surprising that problems slip through. A journal could in theory institute systematic statistical tests on the distribution of sets of data, and that might well catch more falsification than happens at present. The idea has been suggested more than once in the past, but implementation is sporadic.

CHAPTER 5

Quantifying Image Manipulation

5.1 INTRODUCTION

"Seeing is believing" is an old phrase that captures the heart of the problem with image manipulation. Humans are culturally and perhaps also biologically programmed to believe what their eyes tell them. Seeing is our dominant sense and requires less abstraction than language, especially written language, which appeared relatively late in human history. Data require an even further level of abstraction. Many people have trouble with the idea that a series of invisible ones and zeros can have meaning, and that changing just a few of the bits can alter meanings in significant ways. As the saying goes, "it is hard to see" how that could be true.

From an ethnographic viewpoint it is clear that people can look at the same things and see them differently. The native of a tropical forest may look at a tree and see its potential for building, while an educated European may see nothing but greenery. People often see what they want to see. That was the idea behind the story of Potemkin's village, a facade that officials erected to make Catherine the Great of Russia believe the villages she passed through were prosperous. In the U.S. many people in the suburbs believe in widespread prosperity because they do not venture into the poorer sections of urban ghettos. An Australian visitor to a conference in Detroit in the early 2000s spoke with horror about how it resembled a war zone, while locals remarked on how much clean-up had taken place. What people see is not uniformly the same. Image manipulation relies on giving viewers what they expect and want.

This chapter primarily discusses digital images, not because manipulation is impossible with other types of images, as was discussed earlier, but because digital cameras and digital images have become the norm in academic and especially in scientific work, and digital images are much more liable to manipulation. The first part of this chapter will focus on the technology behind digital imaging because understanding the technology is essential to any discussion about how to discover manipulation, how to measure how much manipulation has taken place, and how problematic it is. Images play very different roles in the different disciplines. The humanities generally view images as external to their sources of evidence, which tend to be text based. Some natural sciences use images heavily as evidence, and many social sciences use images as means of expressing quantitative relationships visually. The various disciplines will be discussed separately below.

5.2   DIGITAL IMAGING TECHNOLOGY

5.2.1   BACKGROUND

Blame for the ease of manipulation is often attributed to PhotoShop or occasionally to its GNU (general public license) equivalent, GIMP, but these are merely tools that make the manipulation easier. Anyone who can write programs to manipulate files at the bit level can alter a digital photograph. GIMP itself began as a student project at Berkeley. Seth Burgess explains in his "A brief history of GIMP":

> "A couple of students at Berkeley, Spencer Kimball and Peter Mattis, decided they wanted to write an image manipulation program rather than write a compiler in scheme/lisp for professor Fateman (CS164). Neither one had graphic arts experience, but it seemed like a neat project. They got encouragement from professor Forsythe to implement some new features too—rumor has it intelligent scissors was Spencer's CS280 project." [Burgess, 1998]

Others with comparable programming skills could create their own image manipulation tools, a fact that should be remembered when using tool-specific detection mechanisms to discover manipulation. In almost all cases, it is possible for a skilled person to cover up changes in the file itself, though it may be possible for hardware forensics to recover a deleted and unchanged original on a storage device, if the device is available and sufficient suspicion exists to warrant an investigation.

5.2.2   HOW A DIGITAL CAMERA WORKS

To understand digital image manipulation requires some understanding of how a digital camera works. There is in fact no original image that emerges from the camera itself, only a bitstream that comes from different types of sensors. The image is in most cases the product of software built into the camera. Analog cameras do not give perfect accuracy. Instead of a variety of sensors, analog cameras use different sets of chemicals in a film to react to the light. Different chemicals react more or less quickly to light. For example, black and white silver halide film has modifications to allow it react to different exposure times, and color films have a noticeable variation in color, depending on the manufacturer.

There are two common types of sensors in digital cameras: CCD (charged couple devices) and CMOS (complementary metal-oxide-semiconductor). An explanation of how the devices work can be found on the Teledyne DALSA website. Teledyne DALSA describes itself as: "an international leader in high performance digital imaging and semiconductors…" Here is their explanation:

> "Both types of imagers convert light into electric charge and process it into electronic signals. In a CCD sensor, every pixel's charge is transferred through a very limited number of output nodes (often just one) to be converted to voltage, buffered, and sent

off-chip as an analog signal. All of the pixel can be devoted to light capture, and the output's uniformity (a key factor in image quality) is high. In a CMOS sensor, each pixel has its own charge-to-voltage conversion, and the sensor often also includes amplifiers, noise-correction, and digitization circuits, so that the chip outputs digital bits. These other functions increase the design complexity and reduce the area available for light capture. With each pixel doing its own conversion, uniformity is lower, but it is also massively parallel, allowing high total bandwidth for high speed." [Teledyne, 2016, 2016]

While CCD may seem preferable because of the higher image quality and uniformity, the CCD array has been losing out to CMOS in higher quality digital cameras, partly because of cost, since CMOS is on a single sensor with everything integrated, and CCD requires additional external electronics. The Canon website explains how:

"Canon has overcome this with lateral thinking. Rather than trying to equalise the amplifiers, it has accepted that there will always be a noise pattern. So every time you take a picture, you actually make two exposures—one of the subject, and one with the shutter closed. This second exposure only captures the noise pattern. If the values of this pattern are subtracted from the first exposure, you obtain an image with little or no noise." [Canon Europe, 2016, 2016]

The noise subtraction is done with software, which is the first form of image manipulation. The other problem with CMOS is the physical loss of light because only part of the CMOS is a light sensor and the rest other electronics. Canon explains how they overcome this problem:

"To counteract this, millions of microlenses are used, one over each photo sensor. The microlens covers the photo sensor and the circuitry. Rays of light hitting the edge of the microlens, which would normally be wasted, are now focused on the photo sensor. The effect is to increase the sensitivity of the sensor unit." [Canon Europe, 2016, 2016]

The optics of the camera lens play a role, as do the shutter speed and the focus, and these too affect the bitstream that results in a digital photograph, just as they do for an analog camera. One difference is that older analog cameras required the photographer to make all of the settings by hand, while contemporary digital cameras have automated many of the steps through built-in software. A photographer can override the automatic settings, but the automated choices tend to be better than human choices under normal circumstances.

Two points are important here. One is that the sharpness, brightness, and overall quality of a photograph depend on factors that may significantly alter the nature of the image—not changing the overall shape, but potentially changing discernable features. The second point is that software controls the incoming light stream as well as the final construction of the photograph as it emerges from the camera. Some photographers still prefer a single-lens reflex camera (SLR) because it lets them see the image exactly before the photo is taken, but the image seen through an SLR lens is no more representative of the final product than the screen on typical modern digital cameras. The end-product is a digital manipulation from start to finish.

Cameras used directly with laboratory machines such as microscopes may have their own specific software with settings tuned to the anticipated content. Over time companies may send updates for this software, generally under the heading of improvements, which may be true, but may also mean that the resulting image is subtly different. The broader range of commercial digital cameras have a rich array of settings that affect not only the focus and shutter settings, but also how the software inside the camera interprets the bitstream coming from the sensors. Some settings emulate the effect of ISO 400 film, for example, which was often used for indoor photography such as in museums. Other settings adjust for bright light outdoors or for the use of a flash. Beyond these simple settings are ones for extreme conditions such as a sunset, which shift the color interpretation.

Pet photography is popular and a common option is a fast burst of shots that the software then stitches together into a single derivative photo whose clarity comes through a process that builds sharp lines from the intersection of many less sharp predecessors. With burst mode the autofocus must be on, which is another software decision. Autofocus may be set to look for specific features, such as face recognition or even a smile. Focus in a digital camera is not just a matter of lens adjustment, but of what the software chooses as the primary focus. Scientific photography often involves static objects, but not all living subjects cooperate.

5.2.3   RAW FORMAT

A "raw image format" is generally called a RAW file. The exact structure of the file is hardware-dependent, but the camera makers generally include a header that describes the structure of the file, sensor and image metadata (including standard information about exposure times and other settings), and the data stream itself. A RAW file is sometimes called a digital "negative." It resembles an analog negative in that it is not the final displayable image, but there the resemblance stops. An analog negative can be developed in different ways to produce an image, but is already a fixed product. A RAW file is visible only when a converter program transforms it. The transformer creates a human-viewable copy in a standard format such as TIFF, but retains the full range of data in the RAW file so that people editing an image can manipulate the visible image using RAW file data. The choices for manipulating the image are much broader with a RAW file than with a JPEG or TIFF, because the file retains the full range of light and color information. Katherine Landreth, author of *How to GIMP*, explains what can be done in a blog post called "RAW Photos with GIMP":

> "If a group of pixels in the shadow of your image is totally black, no amount of adjustment is going to bring details back because GIMP and Photoshop don't know anything about that group of pixels other than they started black and you want to make them a lighter color. Hence, the gray blob.

But a RAW file is totally different. It's literally the raw information about the light that your camera recorded with no—or very little—interpretation imposed.

The RAW file contains information about the settings in your camera when you took the photo, so when you open it in a RAW editor you can see the way the photo would look as you shot it. But all of the information the camera had about the light hitting the sensor in that moment is in there too. What that means for you is that you can open that same photo in a RAW editor and literally change the white balance of the photo after you've taken it. Since interpretations of the light aren't fused into the photo." [Landreth, 2016]

In other words, an image that looks like a gray blob can be transformed into a clear photo. It is a matter of choosing the right set of data from the RAW file to make the scene more visible. This is not in any real sense falsification. It is as accurate an interpretation of the actual information reaching the light sensors as would come out from the built-in camera software, but using choices that transform previously invisible or unclear objects. The point is that the range of legitimate manipulation is extremely broad.

Nonetheless the manipulation could also be viewed as similar to conventional natural science or social science data where some data points represent represent outliers that researchers may reasonably discard with an appropriate justification, or may discard because the outliers interfere with a desired result, which would be problematic. The argument in favor of manipulating a RAW file to get a desired result may depend on whether the choice of the image data just enhances the visibility of the image, or actually alters the picture in a way that serves a particular argument.

5.2.4 DISCOVERY ANALYTICS

Tools like Photoshop and GIMP make image manipulation easy, but they tend also to leave tracks that make the changes detectable. Photoshop "Droplets" is a tool that the US Office of Research Integrity recommends to aid those searching for evidence of image manipulation. Understanding how such tools function is important in order to understand what the limits of such tools are. They do not work equally well on all image formats or under all circumstances, and some changes are more easily discovered than others. The simplest example is a JPEG file where someone has copied and pasted content from another JPEG image.

JPEG is the most commonly used output format for digital cameras. All but the most high-end cameras use it, as do many, perhaps most, cameras that are part of scientific devices such as microscopes. JPEG uses a compression algorithm that can lead to a loss of precision and clarity if it is edited and re-saved. TIFF has a lossless compression algorithm that many in the library community favor for long term digital preservation. In broad terms, the way compression works is that the algorithm calculates how many pixels of the same color are in a standard eight by eight segment and transforms that into a calculation. Here is a very simplified example: in a black and white image, eight white pixels in a row might be represented by a vector-like calculation that would expand a white pixel eight times in order to fill the same space. With color images the calculation may provide a gradient that ranges from one end of the color range to another.

Clearly these compression algorithms include some imprecision, and the greater the compression, the more potential for possible error. The compression calculations do not necessarily use only pixels in immediate proximity; they also factor in colors from a broader area. The compression calculation varies from one image to another. The amount of compression in a JPEG tends to be a range rather than a fixed amount. These compression algorithms can be used to detect image manipulation.

Stamm and Liu [2010] explain how they can find traces of image alteration in their article "Forensic detection of image manipulation using statistical intrinsic fingerprints":

> "It is important to note that most image altering operations leave behind distinct, traceable 'fingerprints' in the form of image alteration artifacts. Because these fingerprints are often unique to each operation, an individual test to catch each type of image manipulation must be designed. While detecting image forgeries using these techniques requires performing a large set of operation-specific tests, these methods are able to provide insight into the specific operations used to manipulate an image. Prior work which identifies image tampering by detecting operation specific fingerprints includes the detection of resampling [13], double JPEG compression [14]–[16], as well as the parameterization of gamma correction [17]. Methods for detecting image forgeries have been proposed by detecting local abnormalities in an image's signal-to-noise ratio (SNR) [14]. Additionally, the efficient identification of copy and move forgeries has been studied [18]." [Stamm and Liu, 2010, p. 492]

The authors go on to propose their own approach:

> "In this work, we show that with the exception of the identity mapping, pixel value mappings leave behind statistical artifacts which are visible in an image's pixel value histogram. We refer to these artifacts as the intrinsic fingerprint of a pixel value mapping. By observing the common properties of the histograms of unaltered images, we are able to build a model of an unaltered image's pixel value histogram." [Stamm and Liu, 2010, p. 493]

A statistical approach using such a model helps to give grounds for suspicion, but may not suffice as proof. It is just one indication of the complexity of image manipulation detection.

When a tool copies part of one image to another, it copies the compression information too. This means that a careful examination of an image may be able to detect artifacts of the compression from a different image, even if that image were relatively similar. Metadata in JPEG can be found in the header of a file, but metadata artifacts may also be embedded in other parts of the image file, which can also give an indication of the presence of content that did not come from the original photo. The presence of such tracks represent strong indicators of image manipulation, but their absence may not indicate that no manipulation occurred. A fully uncompressed

TIFF file may show few or no technical artifacts from copying. An edited RAW file will likewise not generally have such artifacts, as long as two RAW files were used and edited with the same software. One of the surest ways to avoid most means for technical detection is to take a new photo of a composite image. The new photo will be a genuine original and have no unexpected compression or metadata artifacts.

Today it is increasingly common for editors to ask for the original photograph as well as the one intended for publication. This makes it possible to uncover manipulation in cases where no deception is intended, and it would be a very naive person who provided evidence that they had copied one image from another. A clever person might well create a fake original and then make entirely acceptable modifications (cropping, for example) to a publication copy to throw off suspicion.

5.2.5   DIGITAL VIDEO

Digital video appeared at roughly the same time as digital photography, and it shares some of the same technology. Just as analog film is largely a sequence of individual still photos, digital video is a stream of digital images that a sensor array captures and turns into a data stream that software must interpret. The speed of video depends on the density of the image, the compression, and the degree to which techniques like interlacing are used, where the camera does not capture whole frames, but alternating lines within the frame that the software then interweaves. By capturing less at any one time, the camera can capture at a greater rate, which improves the smoothness of any motions at the cost of some sharpness.

Software for editing digital video has been around almost as long as software for editing still photographs, and it has many of the same capabilities for brightness, color enhancement, and cropping. It is also possible to cut and paste frames from other videos, a technique that movie-makers use routinely in editing commercial films. Editing an individual frame to add or remove content in the frame itself is harder, because of the need to make the exact same changes in neighboring frames to enable smooth transitions within the sequence. Nonetheless, such editing is certainly possible. The question is whether it is worth the effort.

Many of the image manipulation problems in the sciences rely on the relative ease of static image editing. Video sequences are used less often than static image capture, but tools for capturing digital video have become common in the form of smart phones. The likelihood is that the use of digital video will increase in scholarly journals once they cease to favor static formats like PDF in order to resemble print production. When publishers treat digital video as an integral part of a scholarly publication, the number of cases of video manipulation will likely grow.

Measuring manipulation in digital video is not fundamentally different than with static images. There are tracks that editing systems leave behind that can be discovered at the bit level, and the complexity of timing and transition leaves room for error. Covering up all tracks may be harder, since the equivalent of re-photographing a faked image to create one that is free of editing artifacts is far more challenging. At present, image manipulation in digital video is not a significant issue beyond the occasional controversy about sequences that were edited out.

5.3   ARTS AND HUMANITIES

5.3.1   INTRODUCTION

Digital image manipulation is not generally viewed as a problem in the arts and humanities. There are many examples of manipulation from the era of analog photography, particularly for political images from the Soviet Union. Examples can be found in the chapter by James Oberg [2013], "Cosmonauts who weren't there," and all come from before digital imaging replaced chemical film. It may be that the Soviet-Era image manipulation was so widespread that it undermined the automatic credibility that an official photograph could once command, especially when combined with a widespread awareness of image manipulation tools. Images never played a large role in the more language- and text-oriented humanities, and writers today use them more often as illustrations than evidence. This does not mean that digital images are not manipulated in the humanities or in the arts, but that manipulation is broadly seen as acceptable because of its illustrative character and because, in the end, it is text that matters in humanities scholarship, not images.

An example of how a manipulated image can be used as a form of social commentary appears in Craig Stroupe's chapter on "The Rhetoric of Irritation: Inappropriateness as Visual/Literate Practice":

"To create his composite, Mahlberg used Photoshop to rework Bob Jackson's famous news photo of Jack Ruby assassinating Lee Harvey Oswald in the garage of the Dallas police station on Sunday, November 24, 1963. In Mahlberg's revision, the scene of violence is recast into a rock-and-roll venue, with Jack Ruby lunging forward grasping an electric guitar, Oswald's face contorted into a microphone, and the wide-eyed officer, Jim Leavelle, playing an electric keyboard. The relationships among the three—the assassin's stealthy aggression, the victim's surprise and anguish, the guard's shocked recognition—is rendered by Mahlberg's introduction of the instruments into the intensely coordinated performance of a garage band at a perfect musical moment." [Stroupe, 2004, p. 252]

This is not an attempt to falsify factual information, but to comment on it visually. Photoshop image manipulation plays a positive role as an editing tool. In theory, the altered photo could be used by someone who wanted to dispute the facts of what happened, but that was not the intent. This kind of image manipulation as a form of comment or critique is likely to play an increasing role in the arts and especially among those who use artistic images for social commentary.

5.3.2   ARTS

Image manipulation generally represents a tool in the arts as part of a long history where no one imagined that a painting or a sculpture was a perfect copy of the original person or scene. With photography there was an early public impression that the printed result exactly reproduced the person or scene, but professional photographers were well aware of the amount of thought and work that went into making adjustments to get the final product. The issue today with digital imaging in the arts is less whether some form of manipulation took place than whether the amount of manipulation violates a written rule (as in a contest) or an unwritten rule (as in airbrushing a publicity photo).

One well-known controversy was the *Newsweek* magazine cover photo of the business-woman Martha Stewart as she emerged from prison. Jonathan Glater describes what happened in his article "Martha Stewart Gets New Body in Newsweek":

> "On its cover this week, Newsweek features what appears to be a photo of Ms. Stewart but is actually an image combining a photo of her face and one of a model's body. The idea, an editor at the magazine said, was to portray Ms. Stewart as she may appear when she emerges from prison in a few days—slimmer and stronger than ever." [Glater, 2005]

The *Newsweek* spokesperson claimed that the image was a "photo illustration," and that this was clear in the credits. Nonetheless it violated one of the unwritten rules.

> "Janice E. Castro, director of graduate journalism programs at Medill School of Journalism at Northwestern University, said the image did not look completely artificial and might be mistaken for an unmodified photo. That is cause for some concern, Ms. Castro said. 'If the reader thinks it's a news photo, an actual photograph, as opposed to a piece of art, then you should never change the truth of the photo,' Ms. Castro said." [Glater, 2005]

In this case measuring the falsification was easy because there were actual photos of Martha Stewart to compare with the fake. Nonetheless the situation—a professional-looking photograph on the cover of a nationally known news magazine—likely persuaded many viewers that the picture was real, especially since the photo credit was on page 3.

The World Press Photo Foundation originated in 1955 "when a group of Dutch photographers organized a contest to expose their work" [World Press Photo, 2016b]. Their contest has explicit rules against manipulation: "the content of a picture cannot be altered by adding, rearranging, reversing, distorting or removing people and/or objects from within the frame" [World Press Photo, 2016b]. The exceptions are cropping and removing sensor dust. The contest requires contestants to submit proofs that include the RAW file or the original JPEG and three frames before and after the contest photo; and "[t]wo independent digital analysts compare original files with contest entries to determine whether the content of any picture (either a single picture or frame in a story) has been altered" [World Press Photo, 2016a]. The analysis loads the original and the contest image as layers in Photoshop to detect differences and check the histograms to detect darkening or lightening. The weakness of this process is of course the fact that a contestant could also manipulate the images sent as evidence, and there appears to be no bit-level test to detect alterations.

Digital manipulations are not the only ones forbidden in the contest. Staging a scene is also forbidden, with the exception of portraits. "[A]dding or removing content from the image" counts as manipulation, but "processing by itself," including conversion to grayscale or some color processing, does not count [World Press Photo, 2016a]. These rules are by no means universal for photographic contests, and photography as art increasingly involves manipulation as a creative element in the process. These rules could, however, apply as well to the use of images in the natural and social sciences.

5.3.3   HUMANITIES

Image manipulation becomes image falsification only under circumstances where the image itself serves as evidence, and most of the cases where that seems likely in the humanities today come from the potential for faking sources or manipulating digital images from hard-to-find originals, such as manuscripts, drawings, or paintings. So far there have been no reports of cases involving alterations to a digital image of, for example, a handwritten manuscript to provide support for an academic argument about land donations in medieval Italy. That kind of falsification would be relatively easy to do, if a person could find a hard-to-check source, such as a manuscript in private hands, and were to take a digital picture. One could then edit the manuscript by cutting out words or even by cutting and pasting existing letters to form new words. Scholars who had access to a substantial collection of digital images of manuscripts could create plausible fakes by combining elements from several variants to create a new edition. Today it would not be hard to claim that the original was in a war zone in the Middle East and was stolen, lost, or destroyed.

Since people treat the digital images of texts as genuine, gaining credibility would be easy. The credibility is justifiable because most such manuscripts belong to libraries or public institutions that have a reputation for trustworthiness and have no obvious economic incentive for falsification. The incentive structure could change as more and more academic institutions have to compete for grant resources to keep basic operations going. One safeguard is that any large-scale falsification or forgery would raise suspicions, and then forensic tools would be employed.

A more lucrative option may be false copies of "lost" letters by recently dead and famous authors. A clever forger could take existing handwritten letters, create digital images of the words and individual letters, and arrange them into new sentences. From a new digital composite it would be possible to create a stencil to copy the words onto period paper using period ink. Physical detection would be challenging and the handwriting would be genuine. Discovery could involve checking the exact shape of letters against known handwriting samples to find whether there are too many identical matches, assuming there were enough suspicion to warrant the effort. The best metric for detection in this case may be style, but style is too variable to offer certainty if the job were done well.

In the future the risk of image manipulation in the humanities will likely grow as humanists rely more on digital images as evidence. A field like ethnography is potentially especially vulnerable, since ethnographers tend to use contemporary photographs as part of the evidence they collect. For them still photographs may become less significant than video streams because of the connection between voice and movement that is possible in video. Examples include dance sequences, social interactions, and group interviews. It is also be possible to create a digital version of an analog film and to manipulate it. At this point the rewards for both image and video manipulation in the humanities are so low that the effort is not worthwhile.

5.4   SOCIAL SCIENCES AND COMPUTING

5.4.1   OVERVIEW

The social sciences and computing use a broad range of digital images, many of which are not photographic, but computer-generated diagrams whose purpose is to express large sets of data or numerical results in a compact and readily understandable way. In one sense the problems with image manipulation in these fields are extensions of the kind of data manipulation that was discussed in the previous chapter, with the significant difference that the underlying data are true and the problem is whether the images representing these data mislead the viewer. Enough complexity intrudes in the process that provable falsification is rare and most problems are attributed either to poor judgment by the author or to misunderstanding on the part of the reader.

Any attempt to render large amounts of data into forms that are meaningful to human readers must involve a certain amount of manipulation of both the data and the image. The end result may not be an unbiased original representation, but one that gives an impression supporting a particular argument. Such an image is a very different form of evidence than a photograph whose intent is to capture a fixed record of a particular event at a particular time in an interpretation-free form. Deception need not be involved, any more than a verbal argument in favor of one interpretation implies falsehood. Images generated from data are just different and require manipulation—often significant amounts of manipulation—to be useful at all. The key question is: what boundaries are acceptable?

5.4.2   TRAINING AND VISUALIZATION

Visual judgments depend heavily on training and how readers understand visualization. Within a particular discipline, the researchers may have standard kinds of diagrams that they use, but there is no guarantee that the people from other disciplines will be equally adept at reading those diagrams. Even people within the same discipline may read a diagram more to get an overall impression than to analyze what particular aspects of the diagram represent, and they may focus on certain salient aspects and skip others. This is true in reading text as well, with the difference that for many (but by no means all) people, the visual argument makes a stronger impression. Some kinds of diagrams are easier to read than others. A pie chart or a bar graph are among the simplest and most common. A scatter graph with a line representing the trend of regression line is a meaningful diagram only if the reader knows what a regression line means. For a person without the necessary minimum of statistical background, it is little more than a line with a bunch of random dots.

The assumption that a set of data is easier to understand in a graphic form includes an implicit expectation that the details matter less than an overall impression. The purpose of a diagram is not to focus on individual cases, but to give shape to the whole. In many disciplines this makes sense, because the argument of a paper will depend on convincing the reader that a certain outcome is more (or less) likely than others. This is the goal of the relatively new field called data visualization. The National Science Foundation (NSF) published a report on visualization in 1987 that had significant influence:

> "The NSF Panel on Graphics, Image Processing, and Workstations published its land-mark report Visualization in Scientific Computing in 1987. 'ViSC [visualization in scientific computing] is emerging as a major computer-based field,' the panel wrote. 'As a tool for applying computers to science, it offers a way to see the unseen … [it] promises radical improvements in the human/computer interface.'" [National Science Foundation, 2000, p. 92]

Visualization received significant NSF financial support and encouragement:

> "NSF earmarked funds for visualization at the supercomputing centers from 1990 to 1994. During that time, application of visualization techniques spread. Since 1997, NSF's Partnerships for Advanced Computational Infrastructure (PACI) program has stimulated further advances in areas ranging from sophisticated tools for managing, analyzing, and interacting with very large data sets to collaborative visualization tools to enable researchers from far-flung areas to work interactively on a real-time basis. Applications now span the whole of contemporary science." [National Science Foundation, 2000, p. 92]

This emphasis on visualization had an influence on the tools available for processing data. The standard statistical packages, for example, now offer a wide range of visualization options, all of which count as image generators in the broadest sense. It is possible to depict data in any of a wide range of shapes, sizes, and colors, all of which in some genuine sense accurately represent the data, and all of which in some sense distort it to make a particular point.

Researchers use the various statistical packages to create visualizations today. The statistical packages are relatively old. Any fixed date for the development of a statistical package is somewhat artificial, because the development took place over years of testing and beta versions, but most of the leading packages today came from the 1960s. The oldest was arguably BMDP (BioMedical Data Programs), which Wilfrid Dixon developed at the University of California Los Angeles in 1962 [Glassner and Dixon, 1986]. SPSS (Statistical Package for the Social Sciences) bought BMDP in 1995. Norman Nie at the University of Chicago was one of the early developers of SPSS, now IBM SPSS, which had its initial release in 1968. SAS (Statistical Analysis System) began at North Carolina State University in the later 1960s with a commercial release in 1976. The newest package in broad use is R, a GNU project that came originally from the University of Auckland in New Zealand and that had its initial release in 1992. The age of these packages means that most researchers today have had training on one or more of them. Their age also means that the various releases of commercial versions over time have evolved and that the visualization options have changed over time, so that an older visualization may not reproduce exactly on newer versions of the software.

Hadley Wickham, who works with the R statistical package, discusses the wide range of graphics in his article "A Layered Grammar of Graphics":

> "The most important modern work in graphical grammars is 'The Grammar of Graphics' by Wilkinson, Anand, and Grossman (2005). This work built on earlier work by Bertin (1983) and proposed a grammar that can be used to describe and construct a wide range of statistical graphics. This article proposes an alternative parameterization of the grammar, based around the idea of building up a graphic from multiple layers of data. The grammar differs from Wilkinson's in its arrangement of the components, the development of a hierarchy of defaults, and in that it is embedded inside another programming language." [Wickham, 2012, p. 4]

Some of the elements of the "grammar" are items such as "the basic plot" and layered diagrams (including statistical transformations), which are not complicated for someone trained in statistics, but which involve enough complications that Wickham suggests the "equivalent of a spellchecker" or "a grammar checker … [that] would identify common mistakes and warn the user" [Wickham, 2012, p. 25]. Some of the mistakes include:

> "Too many variables. It is hard to see the relationship between more than three variables in a single panel: two position and one other. … Overplotting. It is easy to draw incorrect conclusions about the distribution of points in the presence of overplotting. … Alphabetical ordering. Categorical variables are often displayed in alphabetical ordering. Wainer (2004) called this mistake 'Alabama first!' due to the propensity for states to be listed in alphabetical order. [And] Polar coordinates. We know that humans are better at judging length than angle or area (Cleveland and McGill 1987), and polar coordinates have a singularity at the origin that makes it difficult to judge angle for objects with small radius." [Wickham, 2012]

These kinds of mistakes represent image manipulations that can cause the reader to misunderstand and misinterpret the research results. It does not imply a problem with the author's integrity, but in some real sense such mistakes undermine the meaning of the underlying data.

5.4.3   STANDARD MANIPULATIONS

Turning data into images through visualization programs requires certain kinds of standard manipulations. These include how the data are sorted, how they are selected, and the kind of diagram to use for display. Sorting is one of the most basic tasks, and can have a significant effect on the display, as Wickham noted above with "Alabama first." Equally common is an ascending or descending order for a particular variable, in which case the choice of the variable tends to mask patterns for other variables. A line graph can show multiple sets of data points and make it possible to contrast them, but a diagram with too many lines can also be hard to read. The size of the intervals on the X and Y axis can also emphasize proximity or differences. The same is true for a logarithmic scale.

An example of a well-intentioned but potentially misleading graphic comes from a researcher comparing features of over 100 institutions using three categorical variables. The work is as yet unpublished and therefore will not be cited, since the final version is likely to be significantly different. The researcher wanted an image that would show each of the categorical variables in relation to each other and in relation to the institution. The categorical variable 1 meant that a condition was present, and 0 meant that it was not. The initial result was three horizontal bar graphs displayed next to each other. The author wanted to emphasize a particular value in the first graph, so the primary sort was by this category and the secondary by the name of the institution. Each category received a color. The researcher then wanted to compare results by institution in the second table, which meant sorting again by the first category and by the institution, but displaying the color of the second category. In terms of the mathematics and the sorting, this all worked well. Multiple horizontal bar graphs stood side by side, and a reader could draw a horizontal line across the page to map all the results for a single institution.

Nonetheless readers had two problems. One was the fineness of the lines, so that it was hard to see an individual result when it differed from blocks of others on either side. The other problem was with the colors themselves: the statistical package did not pick the same colors consistently for the categorical variables 0 and 1, and the researcher did not know how to force a color choice. That meant that the reader could not just assume that orange always meant 0 and blue always meant 1. Even though the legend for the table was clear, readers found it confusing, for example, that green meant 1 in one chart and 0 in another. It made reading the chart horizontally difficult because readers had to adjust the values in their minds for each part. The problem was fixable, but became apparent only in discussion.

Another example comes from a famous paper in the academic accounting literature. Linda Bamber et al. wrote in their article "Do we really 'know' what we think we know? A case study of seminal research and its subsequent overgeneralization":

> "We show that the community of accounting researchers has not fully appreciated the sensitivity of research conclusions to (necessarily) subjective research design choices, and that this failure has led to the subsequent overgeneralization of early evidence." [Bamber et al., 2000, p. 103]

The problem with W. Beaver's prize-winning 1968 article, "The information content of annual earnings announcements," was that many readers did not carry away from this study the carefully nuanced claims in the text and the numerical detail in the tables, but the simple and dramatic graphs, which showed the stock market reacting sharply to firms' announcements of their annual earnings.

In fact, as Bamber et al. write, the typical stock market reaction to earnings announcements does not look like the representation in the graphs. Such sharp reactions occur only for some firms, and these firms dominate the graphs (though not the stock market) for two reasons. First, because Beaver wanted to see market reactions to earnings announcements, not to other news, he excluded from the sample those firms for which other important news was announced at the same time as earnings. This was a reasonable choice and was carefully explained in Beaver's study; but it had the effect of biasing the sample toward firms for which there was generally little news available, and which therefore would tend to have large market reactions to earnings. Readers who carried away only the dramatic graph in their minds did not necessarily carry away the information in Beaver's text that identified the bias.

Second, and perhaps more interesting from the point of view of data-summarization choices, the dramatic form of the graphs is created by the fact that they use means rather than other possible summary measures to represent a large body of data—and with data like those in the Beaver study, the means can give a misleading picture. The large mean market reactions are created by a minority of very large reactions combined with a majority of reactions that are not significantly different from zero. Thus, as Bamber et al. point out, the typical reaction (near zero) and the mean reaction (large) are quite different. Because means are the focus of much statistical testing, it seems natural to use them in graphic summaries, but they can be misleading when they obscure important within-sample differences.[1]

5.5   BIOLOGY

5.5.1   LEGITIMATE MANIPULATIONS

Biology uses photographic images in particular as evidence. Many of these images come from cameras attached to machines that enable researchers to view information at a level of magnification that would be invisible to the naked eye. The use of cameras with, for example, microscopes long predated the advent of digital imaging. With analog film a scientist needed developing room skills that were not an ordinary part of their training, but by the time computer imagery became well established, no respectable scientist lacked the basic computing skills necessary to install and run a package like Photoshop or GIMP. More importantly the line between legitimate manipulation and falsification became more unclear as the options for legitimate manipulation grew.

Thorsten Beck's book *Shaping Images* examines these boundaries as part of the research project "Bild Wissen Gestaltung" (Image Knowledge Shaping) at Humboldt-Universität zu

---

[1] I am grateful to Joan Luft, whose research area is this, for explaining the case to me.

Berlin. He reports interviews with more than one scientist who openly discussed what they considered to be acceptable manipulation. Here is one example:

> "She reports how she once took the intact side of a museum object (a crab) and replaced the damaged parts in Photoshop. But that was a 'grey area.' One is allowed to do this, as long as one is not working with a holotype specimen, or with a cataloged object. She shakes her head as if she intends to distance herself from such practices and repeats that today she would refrain from doing this, because valuable information about the specimen could get lost, like the asymmetry of claws. She looks straight at me and emphasizes, I would not do that any more, I would rather live with it if a leg is missing somewhere—even if that does not look good." [Beck, 2016, p. 162]

In this case the photograph is more of an illustration than evidence, and the goal is not to make an argument on the basis of Photoshop changes, but to give the reader a complete picture of what the crab looked like. Her reluctance about doing the same repair job today offers an indication of how much stricter the rules for image manipulation have become, even for cases where nothing of significance is being falsified.

Another example comes from a marine biologist, who must take the condition of the water and the background into account in photographs. Beck describes his interview with her.

> "... it is the influence of water that comes to her mind when referring to aspects of the invisible. Often she takes pictures of the organisms in water and then she instantly ran into problems like clouding or reflections from the glass that obscured the view. Even when taking the organism out of the water its wet surface causes problems. It is possible to retouch this with Photoshop, but the water still remains the 'invisible opponent.' Background is another problem. It is not originally 'invisible,' she explains, but replacing the background helped to produce a clear contrast for the object. In an ideal case it is possible to 'crop' the organism, but often she simply darkens the color of the background to generate an optimal visibility of the organism." [Beck, 2016, p. 118]

The issue here is how to make the part of the image that is actual evidence—namely the organism—clear without distorting it. A completely unedited image would not constitute better or more honest evidence. Leaving the clouding and reflections from the water in the image would force the reader to remove them mentally, which would not necessarily lead to a more reliable interpretation. The danger of altering some important feature when removing the clouding and reflections is real, and a scientist who describes the editing process in detail could still intend deception, but the removal could be a reasonable trade-off for clarity.

Background changes may represent a larger-scale invasiveness, because such alterations may affect more of the image. Changing the background color increases the contrast so that some features of the image become clearer and more salient. A similar increase in contrast for the organism itself would raise more concern about the degree of manipulation without necessarily having a different effect. One concern about background color alteration is that it changes the impression of the organism's environment, which could also influence the overall impression on the reader. Most of the rules about manipulating scientific images focus strictly on the object of the picture, while professional photographers and artists are well aware that the environment around the object matters as well.

Cropping is in some sense also a background change, since it removes extraneous content. Virtually all journals allow cropping, as do photo contests, even though cropping represents a potentially radical alteration of the image as a whole. The logic for allowing cropping is that it does not alter the view of the object of interest, which is reasonable as long as the environment has no subtle effect on the perception of the image. For example, the perception of a photo of a single example of a one-celled organism may be different than the perception of that same type when the photograph includes several variants, since even two one-celled organisms are not necessarily identical.

A popular solution for testing the degree and veracity of a scientific image is to ask scientists to provide the version of the image as it came from the camera along with the publication version, so that the editors can judge for themselves how legitimate the editing was. While this solution for discovery is reasonable, it obscures an important set of metrics: first, to what degree do even acceptable changes such as cropping alter the perception of the content; and second, to what degree does banning certain manipulations also obscure details that matter for a reasonable judgment of the content. One solution is for journals to publish both the edited and unedited versions of images, which has little or no cost in the world of digital publishing. Many journals and their policies are, however, still mentally trapped by the limitations of paper publication.

5.5.2 ILLEGITIMATE MANIPULATIONS

Some well-documented cases of image fraud have less to do with image manipulation than with passing off images of one thing as another. The U.S. Office of Research Integrity gives an example in its "Case Summary: Li, Zhiyu" (20 July 2016):

> "ORI found that the Respondent intentionally, knowingly, and recklessly engaged in research misconduct by falsely claiming to have generated recombinant Clostridium perfringens (Cp) strains, Cp/sod-, Cp/sod-/PVL, and Cp/plc-/sod-/PVL, to depict the effects of recombinant Cp strains on their ability to destroy cancer cells in a murine model, when these bacterial strains were not produced nor the data derived from them, ..." [Office of Research Integrity, 2016]

The manipulation in this case was intended to hide the condition of the tissue before and after treatment by substituting images that were not part of the test:

> "Respondent trimmed and used a portion of a figure that was reported as mouse pancreatic tumor tissue treated with control liposomes in four (4) figures (Figure 6D in R21 CA120017 Final Progress Report, Figure 10D in R01 CA130897-01 A1, Fig-

ure 7D in R01 CA130897-01 A2, and Figure 5D in R01 CA148697-01), to represent results from mouse pancreatic tumor tissue not treated with control liposomes ..." [Office of Research Integrity, 2016]

The basic problem is that such images are hard even for experts to read, and the claim that a particular image represented results after the researcher had treated tissue with a chemical, when in fact it had not been treated, was plausible enough on the face of it that it went through the review process and was published. This kind of fraud could occur with an analog image as well.

The tight link between image manipulation and data manipulation is clear in the case of a paper by Nicolás Herranz et al. entitled "Lysyl Oxidase-like 2 Deaminates Lysine 4 in Histone H3" in the journal *Molecular Cell*. The case was reported in Retraction Watch by Dalmeet Singh Chawla on 29 June 2016. The authors themselves requested the retraction and made the following statement as part of the retraction notice, which is printed in full in Retraction Watch:

> "Readers raised concerns about data presented in Figures 1, 3, and 4. We provided all of the raw data corresponding to these figures to Molecular Cell and the Scientific Integrity Committee of our institute, the IMIM (Hospital del Mar Medical Research Institute). The journal and the Scientific Integrity Committee of the IMIM found several issues, but determined that apart from the instance in Figure 3C, there was no evidence of intentional misconduct. However, because the data in the H3K4me3 blot in the left (LOXL2) panel of Figure 3C were inappropriately manipulated, resulting in a figure that does not accurately represent the data as obtained, we are retracting the paper." [Chawla, 2016]

Images based on data are as important as photographic images in biology papers because they are the most convincing way in which researchers can produce readily comprehensible summaries of large amounts of data. In this case the manipulation appears to have been a selection issue, rather than data falsification.

The reuse of images appears often in Retraction Watch reports. In such cases the actual images may be untouched, and the manipulation consists in the fact that they come from sources that have no connection to the current experiment. With complex scientific images this kind of substitution is plausible because the variation in characteristics may be hard to identify without the help of software. Retraction Watch writer Shannon Palus wrote about an example on 3 June 2016 where a journal retracted an article 15 years later after using image analysis software. The retraction notice in the journal states:

> "This article has been withdrawn by the authors. Errors were identified in several figures. Evaluation by the Journal with image analysis software determined that images were reused to represent different experimental conditions in the β-catenin immunoblot in Fig. 2, the β-catenin immunoblots in Fig. 5, the E-cadherin immunoblot in Fig. 6A, the Tcf-4 immunoblot in Fig. 6B, and the β-catenin immunoblot in Fig. 7B. The raw data are no longer available to validate the information. The authors

have expressed the opinion that none of these errors affect the final conclusions of this article that, according to them, have been extensively validated during these 15 years." [Palus, 2016]

The argument that the false images did not affect the conclusions could imply that the evidence in the images was not essential to the logic, or could be mere face-saving. While the latter is more likely, it raises the question of whether authors may supply certain images because they think editors and reviewers expect them, rather than that they contain essential data. In the natural sciences images are rarely treated as decorative non-essentials, but it is possible to imagine a person writing under time pressure deciding to include non-essential and non-genuine images after realizing that the absence of an image could hurt chances for being accepted for publication. Even in the natural sciences, social factors cannot be excluded.

5.6   MEDICINE

5.6.1   LIMITS

The technology and issues for image manipulation in medical research are not fundamentally different than for biology, but the stakes are higher because of the human consequences if medical practitioners and medical researchers rely on conclusions based on faked data. The U.S. Office of Research Integrity has a focus by law specifically on public health research. The mission of the Office on its web page states:

> "Specifically, the Notice is to reflect that the Assistant Secretary for Health (ASH) will make proposed findings of research misconduct and administrative actions in response to allegations of research misconduct involving research conducted or supported by components of the Public Health Service (PHS) ..." [Office of Research Integrity, 2000]

Most standards of proof are higher for medical research. In statistical tests, for example, the usual expectation in medical research is $p < 0.005$ rather than $p < 0.05$, as in the social sciences. This could reasonably suggest that the metrics for falsification or manipulation should be an order of magnitude more strict than for other biological research. That is not the same as just imposing stricter rules without a clear measure of what the stricter rule means. Statistical probability measures have a specific meaning: one chance in 20 or one chance in 200 of being wrong. Allowing cropping or banning repair to an obscured part of an image are not steps on a continuum, but discrete actions with unmeasured independent consequences.

Cell Press (2016) offers a number of guidelines for image processing under "Information for Authors":

> "In the case of image processing, alterations must be applied to the entire image (e.g., brightness, contrast, color balance). In rare instances for which this is not possible (e.g., alterations to a single color channel on a microscopy image), any alterations

must be clearly stated in the figure legend and in the Experimental Procedures section." [Cell Press, 2016]

This sounds on the face of it like a very reasonable restriction, but it could also have consequences for how an image is read, if the brightness, contrast, or color balance changes make one part of an image more (or less) visible, even though the likely intent of the rule is to ensure equal treatment to all parts of the image. A more precise policy could include the amount of change allowed. Photoshop and GIMP provide specific measures.

The guidelines continue:

"Groupings and consolidation of data (e.g., cropping of images or removal of lanes from gels and blots) must be made apparent and should be explicitly indicated in the appropriate figure legends." [Cell Press, 2016]

There are two ways to do cropping. One is with the camera focus and the other is with software. For many microscopes and similar machines the focus is relatively inflexible, but that does not mean that a researcher cannot zoom in on one aspect to the exclusion of others. That has the same effect as software-based cropping. Once again the guidelines give a general rule with no metrics. How much cropping is allowed could, for example, be expressed in a percentage of the image as a whole. A 1% cropping is radically different than a 90% cropping. The words "apparent" and "explicitly" do not imply or require concrete measures.

The guidelines also address images created from data:

"Data comparisons should only be made from comparative experiments, and individual data should not be utilized across multiple figures. In cases in which data are used multiple times (e.g., multiple experiments were performed simultaneously with a single control experiment), this must be clearly stated within each figure legend. In the event that it is deemed necessary for proper evaluation of the manuscript, authors will be required to make the original unprocessed data available to the editors of the journal." [Cell Press, 2016]

The focus here is on the specific issue of data reuse in circumstances where the data may come from different experiments. The words "simultaneously" and "single control experiment" are quite explicit, but give no option for situations where, for example, the control was the same, but the experiments were more serial than simultaneous. Truly simultaneous actions are sometimes hard to achieve and the guidelines leave authors to interpret the amount of leeway for themselves.

Metrics for image manipulation are difficult to set in part because the scholarly and scientific community so far has relatively little experience with measuring the implications. This situation is likely to improve over time, once the practice of applying formal metrics to image manipulation gains acceptance.

5.6.2   CASE 1

Medical research gets an unusual amount of attention in Retraction Watch. As of 3 August 2016 it lists 1,076 retractions in the category "clinical study retractions" out of 2,424 for all subjects, or 44%. A number of the retractions involve "western blots," for which the Wikipedia article "Western blot" (2016-07-29T20:17:32Z) gives a relatively non-technical explanation:

> "The western blot (sometimes called the protein immunoblot) is a widely used analytical technique used in molecular biology to detect specific proteins in a sample of tissue homogenate or extract. It uses gel electrophoresis to separate native proteins by 3-D structure or denatured proteins by the length of the polypeptide. The proteins are then transferred to a membrane (typically nitrocellulose or PVDF), where they are stained with antibodies specific to the target protein.[1][2] The gel electrophoresis step is included in western blot analysis to resolve the issue of the cross-reactivity of antibodies." [Wikipedia, 2016]

Manipulating the western blot images can validate (or invalidate) experimental data. One well known case involves Ricky Malhotra, who "admitted to fabricating 74 experiments, and falsifying well over 100 Western blots while at the Universities of Michigan (UM) and Chicago (UC)" according to Retraction Watch [Chawla, 2016]. The Office of Research Integrity adds specifics in its "Case Summary: Malhotra, Ricky":

> "ORI found that Respondent reused and falsely relabeled Western blot gel images, falsified the related densitometry measurements based on the falsified Western blots, and falsified and/or fabricated data for experiments that were not performed." [Office of Research Integrity, 2016]

Reuse and false labeling are among the easiest ways to manipulate images in effect without having to edit the images and run the risk of image-checking software catching the change. This kind of falsification works in part because the western blots are not easy to read and interpret. There is in fact free western blot analysis software to help researchers interpret them, which is an indication of the level of complexity. One way to discover reuse and potentially false labeling is to check the metadata information in the image headers. The metadata should contain date and time stamps that could be a clue if the image comes from too far in the past. Where the time-boundary should be set depends on what the experiment could reasonably have started, and this can be measured as part of other data in most experiments.

5.6.3   CASE 2

The problem with image manipulation is not always with the researcher. Shannon Palus of Retraction Watch reports on a case where the software was at fault in making an image appear as if tampering took place:

"In 2014, we reported that Biochemical Journal had retracted a paper on suspicion it contained 'shoddy Photoshopping'—someone appeared to have blacked out a control lane in one figure. Now there's evidence that it wasn't done on purpose: An investigation at Duke into eight papers, including the Biochemical Journal paper, did not find evidence of misconduct; lead author Paul Kuo, currently chair of surgery at Loyola Medicine, told us that a glitch in the software caused the black box. Nevertheless, the journal does not plan to un-retract the paper." [Palus, 2016]

The journal was apparently not convinced. Retraction Watch quotes the "editor in chief of *Biochemical Journal*, David Carling":

"Whilst we appreciate this possibility, unfortunately, the authors were unable to provide the original image prior to software processing. The authors did send us a gel in which they had re-analysed the original samples, but the quality of this image was extremely poor and it was not possible to draw any firm conclusions from the re-analysis. After careful consideration, we concluded that without the original pre-processed image there were no grounds for changing the retraction notice." [Palus, 2016]

There are several issues at stake here. One is whether the software contained a flaw that manipulated the image in ways the author did not intend, or whether the author made an innocent (if possibly stupid) error in using the software. Retraction Watch quotes the software developer Wayne Rasband:

"This glitch is due to a misunderstanding of how ImageJ works. Unlike some other programs, pressing the backspace key in ImageJ does not delete the selection box. Instead, it is a shortcut for the Edit>Clear command, which erases the contents of the selection box to the background color (usually black). I have attached the section of the ImageJ Users Guide that describes the Clear command. To prevent the selection box from being inadvertently cleared, the gel analyzing function in the latest version of ImageJ (1.51b10) disables this shortcut." [Palus, 2016]

Rasband's explanation makes it clear how the author could have made the error, and seems to find the likelihood of human error plausible enough to have changed the shortcut in subsequent versions. That addresses the smoking pistol reason for the retraction, but the journal editor remained unsatisfied for reasons that had to do with other metrics, among them image quality. An image that is essentially unreadable could in theory be replaced by one that was readable. The authors apparently did not do this, and could not supply the "original pre-processed image," which could be due to poor housekeeping practices, or could be deliberate. Lost images can often be retrieved on a computer if they are merely stored in the wrong place or accidentally deleted. The effort an author is willing to take to recover originals may be a metric worth considering.

This case in particular makes it clear that medical researchers (and others in the natural sciences) often rely on software to help them to interpret the information content of an image.

ImageJ is only one of many programs designed to analyze scientific images at the bitstream and pixel level. Schneider et al. describes this development in the article "NIH Image to ImageJ: 25 years of image analysis":

> "One of the fields in which scientific computing has made particular inroads has been the area of biological imaging. The modern computer coupled to advances in microscopy technology is enabling previously inaccessible realms in biology to be visualized. Although the roles of optical technologies and methods have been well documented, the role of scientific imaging software and its origins have been seldom discussed in any historical context." [Schneider et al., 2012, p. 671]

This kind of analysis software introduces an additional factor in any measurement of image manipulation, because one more software tool is involved that could manipulate or simply misinterpret the image. The likelihood of widely used software misinterpreting image data seems small, but there is already evidence of problems in some areas. Eklund et al. tested several commonly used packages for interpreting brain-mapping data and found that they tended to turn out a lot of false positives. There were two reasons. One was dubious choices in the statistical modeling for many programs; the other was a software bug in one fairly widely used program:

> "… a 15-year-old bug was found in 3dClustSim while testing the three software packages (the bug was fixed by the AFNI group as of May 2015, during preparation of this manuscript). The bug essentially reduced the size of the image searched for clusters, underestimating the severity of the multiplicity correction and overestimating significance (i.e., 3dClustSim FWE P values were too low)." [Eklund et al., 2016]

This is just one more case where it is a mistake to let oneself believe that an image is a true representation of reality. Today software not only creates an image, but may tell the researcher what it means or may potentially mislead the researcher.

5.7 OTHER NATURAL SCIENCES

Photographic images play a role in sciences other than biology and medicine, but fewer reports appear about them in news sources like Retraction Watch. One reason may be that the editors and peer reviewers from other branches of the natural sciences are less aware of image manipulation and of how to discover it, or there may be fewer cases because fewer researchers manipulate images in ways considered to be improper. The latter may be due to different rules, possibly looser or possibly more flexible, or it may be because the rewards for publication are lower. It could also be that the way researchers in the field handle data may make forms of fraud more difficult, as noted above about the lab sciences. Nonetheless, some cases do appear.

Sharon Palus of Retraction Watch reported on a case involving micro/nano-structured materials where "the authors couldn't provide back-up for a figure that contained signs of manipulation." The retraction notice gives more detail about the retraction:

"Following information that Figure 1 in this publication (see the picture on top) may have been manipulated, further investigation revealed that the nanoparticles are pixel for pixel the same in every instance, suggesting that they are the same nanoparticle image-copied and pasted. Certain nanoparticles have a harsh white boundary at the bottom right corner independent of whether they are located on top of another nanoparticle or on the background image. Finally, an image integrity check (bottom picture) established significant differences in noise levels between the nanoparticles and the background." [Palus, 2016] (Koneswaran, retraction notice, 2016)

The report suggests the application of several metrics in this case. One is the degree to which the particles are absolutely identical. A non-expert would likely not be aware of how much difference should exist, and the normal degree of difference would be important to know as part of the measure. Even the editor seems uncertain. The white boundary at the bottom corner could represent a light source. How much variation should be expected is a relevant question. The noise-level differences offer a convincing argument, since noise-level information comes from the photosensors, and having differences strongly suggests two separate photos.

Image manipulation is sometimes done so crudely that it is relatively easy to detect. Cat Ferguson of Retraction Watch reported on a case and quoted from a summary of the official report by Jeffrey Botkin, the University of Utah's research integrity officer:

"The manipulation consisted of a cut and paste "patch" over two relatively small areas of the image. These manipulations represent data falsification. For the ACSNano publication, the Investigation Committee could not determine a rationale for the image manipulation as the 'patches' did not appear to cover significant data elements in the image." [Ferguson, 2014]

The guilty person was a graduate student who had been assisting a professor, which raises the question of why neither the professor nor the peer reviewers caught a crude manipulation, unless the reason is in fact that the manipulations did not affect "significant data elements" and therefore were not considered carefully. People notoriously concentrate on the information they want to see.

There is a famous experiment by Daniel Simons called the "The Monkey Business Illusion" where "someone in a gorilla suit walks into the scene, turns to the camera, and beats his chest a few times, then walks off" without most viewers noticing because they are so engaged in the task of counting how often players wearing white are passing a basketball [Golus, 2016]. Interestingly enough the background curtain also changes color, and few notice that either. It seems possible that something similar happened here, where the people reviewing the paper only saw what they wanted to see.

5.8 DETECTION TOOLS AND SERVICES

One of the important services that the U.S. Office of Research Integrity provides is to make detection tools available. Automated detection tools are less likely than humans to ignore an obvious crude manipulation, but such tools are hard to build. Most concentrate on technical clues with the images. The ORI offers a number of tools, most prominently "forensic droplets" for Photoshop:

> "This Droplet simply applies Histogram Equalization, which may reveal areas of erasure in dark areas, or areas of whitening in bright areas. The process is most effective if the contrasting borders can be first cropped from the image, and restricting the 'set-up' area to an area where the range of intensities is reduced." [Office of Research Integrity, 2012]

It is clear from this description that the forensic droplets are not a general tool and that it works best under somewhat restricted circumstances. ORI described its forensic tools as follows:

> "These tools have extended features that will be more useful to institutional committees who are assessing image evidence in their inquiries and investigations. In particular, some of these Forensic Actions utilize 'Adjustment Layers' that allow reexamination of the result of a forensic test retrospectively. The original image is retained (and recoverable), since all changes are made only in the separate overlying layers that superimpose commands which can be modified or rearranged. The size of the image file is increased, but each additional layer preserves a detailed record the analytic step that is resident within forensic test. Results are easier to share." [Office of Research Integrity, 2012]

An important feature of these tools appears to be having access to the original, which may not always be available, or may itself be manipulated to defeat a publicly available test. ORI gives surprisingly few technical details about these tools, perhaps as a protection against those who would find ways to undermine the test. The tools are relatively easy to install and use. Their use seems to be limited, however, and the ORI offers some caveats about how to interpret the results. The first caveat has to do with the fact that false positives can occur and urges caution:

> "A discrepancy in the image should not be conflated with a finding of falsification of data or, for that matter, of Research Misconduct. Making those distinctions require additional fact-finding." [Office of Research Integrity, 2012]

The second caveat is a reminder to compare images with the original data, in the hope that the original data are available and have not themselves been manipulated.

> "Resolution of those questions requires inspection of the original data. However, in the case where an image lacks authenticity, the absence of the original data can be

used as evidence of possible research misconduct and sufficient justification to conduct further fact finding." [Office of Research Integrity, 2012]

The final caveat is probably the most important, because the details of how the instruments worked and how the experiment was conducted can affect any judgment about intentional falsification.

"The interpretation as to whether any image manipulation is serious requires familiarity with the experiment(s) and imaging instruments." [Office of Research Integrity, 2012]

Many other tools exist other than those the ORI recommends on its website. Some are simple, such as one to look at the hidden metadata for Photoshop or other editor tracks. Another is called Fotoforensics (`http://fotoforensics.com/`) and gives a detailed explanation about what is involved in its "error level analysis":

"JPEG images use a lossy compression system. Each re-encoding (resave) of the image adds more quality loss to the image. Specifically, the JPEG algorithm operates on an 8x8 pixel grid. Each 8x8 square is compressed independently. If the image is completely unmodified, then all 8x8 squares should have similar error potentials. If the image is unmodified and resaved, then every square should degrade at approximately the same rate. ELA saves the image at a specified JPEG quality level. This resave introduces a known amount of error across the entire image. The resaved image is then compared against the original image. If an image is modified, then every 8x8 square that was touched by the modification should be at a higher error potential than the rest of the image. Modified areas will appear with a higher potential error level." [Office of Research Integrity, 2012]

Metrics based on the compression data can be fairly specific both about location and about the amount of manipulation, and resaving the image to expose changes is a clever use of the JPEG compression algorithm. The software builds on the compression information with analysis of the luminance and chrominance values, which are also part of the JPEG encoding. Unfortunately these approaches work only with JPEG files.

Computer-based testing of images is not the only or even the ideal solution. Alison McCook interviewed Mike Rossner, former editor of the *Journal of Cell Biology*, for Retraction Watch. He argues for a more systematic pre-publication image screening and has set up a company called "Image Data Integrity"[2] to provide consulting services in the area. McCook lists several other consultants as well, including Alan Price's "Price Research Integrity Consultant Experts"[3] and Jana Christopher's "Image Integrity."[4] Rossner explained his approach in an article called "How to Guard Against Image Fraud," which resembles the ORI analysis that makes use of

---

[2]`http://www.imagedataintegrity.com/`
[3]`http://researchmisconductconsultant.com/`
[4]`http://image-integrity.com/`

JPEG compression. Richard Van Noorden wrote about Christopher's work in an interview called "The image detective who roots out manuscript flaws." Christopher explains her work as follows:

> "I check to see if micrographs, photographs and data we typically publish, such as western blots and gels, are duplicated or illicitly manipulated—flipped, rotated, inserted, cropped, duplicated, spliced or otherwise digitally altered. I use tools provided by the US Office of Research Integrity that work with Photoshop: they allow you in a semi-automated procedure to adjust the contrasts and settings to highlight flaws." [Van Noorden, 2015]

Once again the detection approach relies heavily on artifacts in the JPEG compression algorithm that help to reveal manipulation. Christopher is aware of the limitations:

> "I'm very aware of the limitations. If someone really tries to cheat and they cheat well, it's unlikely that we would see that. But most of what we find are genuine mistakes, which we prevent from entering the scientific literature." [Van Noorden, 2015]

Clearly these detection tools and the services that use them go a long way toward discovering image manipulation in scientific and scholarly articles if editors and reviewers will use the tools or services systematically. That fact is, however, as Jana Christopher said, that someone who is aware of the tools and has enough technical knowledge can take steps to circumvent existing discovery tools. Catching genuine mistakes is of real value too, and probably includes the majority of the cases, but the question remains how much intentional fraud lurks undiscovered in the scholarly literature.

5.9   CONCLUSION

Image manipulation is particularly an issue for the medical and biological sciences today, because a number of well-known cases have increased awareness. The focus on image manipulation has sharpened since the U.S. Congress set up the Office of Research Integrity in 1985, whose general mission is broad, but whose focus is by law on research related to public health. This focus has driven much of the tool development as well as the services involving those tools, as was discussed above. While this focus has benefited the scientific community with specific metrics involving JPEG compression, it has done relatively little to help in identifying fraud using other formats in other academic disciplines.

One of the important factors in making judgments about when image manipulation becomes fraud involves understanding the human motivations and social circumstances in which the manipulation occurs. The easy answer is to assume that fraud occurs when the authors feel serious pressure to improve their financial or social status. That is certainly a factor, but many who engage in fraudulent image manipulation have plenty of money and respect. Weariness, laziness, worry about losing the admiration of colleagues after many successes all play a potential role. Image manipulation fraud defines simple profiling.

There seems to be evidence that a large number of manipulations had no clear fraudulent intent. Some were clearly mistakes, some were probably cases where the boundary between acceptable and unacceptable manipulation was unclear. These boundaries have changed over time and are not uniform across all journals or disciplines. The extreme cases are clear, such as duplicating parts of an image or using images from different experiments. The number of known cases of image manipulation with the intent to deceive remains relatively small compared to the population of those being published, but discovery remains a problem.

As was discussed at the beginning of the chapter, it is technically feasible to create a manipulated image that existing tools cannot readily detect. It is also possible to alter the original data stream so that comparisons become hard or impossible to detect. A person with the right technical knowledge and skills can become a successful forger. In the natural sciences the one really safe way to make sure that no manipulation has occurred is a completely independent replication of the experiment from the start.

The problem with replications is that they take time and resources, and people who do replications get very little academic credit for the effort unless they find a discrepancy—which also means that anyone who gets a different result must invest more time and trouble to show that they did not make an error themselves. Reasonable incentives to undertake this kind of work simply do not exist. From the point of view of the good of society as a whole, replicating every experiment may also not be justified when it comes at the expense of new discoveries. That means, however, that errors inevitably creep into the scholarly record. From a historical perspective, that is nothing new.

In addition to the detection tools that the ORI provides or that are available commercially, partial replication can play a role, in so far as that is feasible. Partial replication can mean taking an original data stream (assuming it is the original unedited version) and recreating either the photographic image or other forms of visualization used in a paper. This is a reasonable compromise, as is comparing original and edited images, at least in circumstances where there is no intention to deceive.

Some journals send all images through a set of tests, or hire companies to do it, in order to discover image manipulation. Even more publishers send all articles through a plagiarism check. Such equal treatment for all authors has much to be said for it, even though it leads to a need for expert interpretation when the results land in a gray zone. There is relatively little discussion about the error rates for image-manipulation detection tools, even though essentially all tools caution against overly simple conclusions. In the end some discussion with authors of the images is often necessary to understand what really happened.

CHAPTER 6

Applying the Metrics

6.1 INTRODUCTION

The previous chapters looked at how to discover and measure three specific kinds of research integrity violation: plagiarism, data falsification and manipulation, and image falsification and manipulation. The chapters also looked at the differences among the humanities, social sciences, and natural sciences. This short chapter takes a different approach. Its purpose is to build on the available metrics—some of which are very limited—to consider how to make more reliable and more precise judgments. This chapter divides the discussion into three parts. The first looks at how to detect the gray zones in any particular work, because any investigation must start there. The second looks more closely at where within the range of gray falsification begins. And the third section discusses prevention, not from an ethics viewpoint, but in terms of mechanisms that publishers and institutions can put in place to discourage falsification.

6.2 DETECTING GRAY ZONES

Gray zones are most visible when clear comparisons are possible, as is the case with plagiarism. While it is not true yet that all text is available online, enough is available to make it possible to discover most simple forms of copying with tools like iThenticate that mine text and search for matches. Matches are not hard to find. Mark Ford writes in his review "I Gotta Use Words":

> "Like Sweeney, every poem has got to use words, and those words will also necessarily have been used in the work of earlier or contemporary writers." [Ford, 2016]

The reference is to T. S. Eliot's poem "Sweeney Agonistes" and Eliot himself was famously accused of plagiarism because of his many literary references. Many scholars in the humanities put great weight on the uniqueness of expression, but one factor that makes Eliot's poetry strikingly unique is the way he plays on the intellectual evocations of famous words and phrases. What Eliot does is certainly some distance into a gray zone, or at least could well be for a first-year student writing an essay, but has nothing to do with fraud. Footnotes help separate the zones of gray, and Eliot annotated the American book version of his poem "The Waste Land":

> "… partly, as he recalled in "The Frontiers of Criticism" (1956), with a view to spiking the guns of critics of my earlier poems who had accused me of plagiarism." [Ford, 2016]

Footnotes by authors are, however, rare in poetry or in other non-scholarly creative works (though there are exceptions). They are only one element in the metrics of plagiarism, but are for many a decisive metric. The most common metric is the percentage of matches, which can be adjusted to include longer or shorter passages and to include or exclude bibliographies. What the metrics do not do is to adjust for common phrases and standard scientific phrases, or for the location in an article. Even though the metrics are crude, they serve as an indicator that gray zone issues exist.

The metrics for data falsification are less well developed, in part because there is no large body of public data to use for comparison. This is changing as pressure grows in the scholarly community for authors to publish their data along with their articles. Nonetheless the issue for data falsification is not generally copying data from others but altering the original data to give better results. When the original data are available, comparisons are possible and standardized metrics can apply, such as those in statistics for the inclusion or exclusion of outliers. Someone who genuinely wants to deceive is, however, unlikely to make unaltered original data available, which makes the metrics much cruder. Detecting cases where the original data may be false requires plausibility judgments.

In psychology, as discussed above, there are proposals for statistical tools that check the plausibility of data sets. This approach has the virtue of concrete results, but like many metrics has the potential for false positives (and negatives), as well as a vulnerability to data forgers who reverse-engineer the statistical tools to make their data inconspicuous. An undervalued but important metric is the provenance of the data: data must come from somewhere, and the details about where they were collected, how they were collected, and who was involved contribute to another form of plausibility test. Stories that are too facile come with too few details should raise questions about credibility of the provenance. Claims of confidentiality or data protection need not be absolute. An editor or a designated trusted person within a publishing house could get and test confidential or sensitive information with the promise that it will be handled in legal and acceptable ways. In the humanities text-based sources of data have long been publicly available in libraries and archives, and claims of secret new sources are viewed with suspicion. Similar approaches can improve the metrics for detecting data falsification in other fields.

The metrics for image manipulation are well developed for those using the JEPG format and JPEG compression. With existing tools it is possible to see where color and brightness were changed, and where copying took place. Under proper circumstances these metrics can show what and how much changed, even without the originals for comparison. Other clues can help too, but they depend on the discipline, the kind of image, and the quality of the manipulation. In an ordinary journalistic style photograph, shadows and background inconsistencies can reveal manipulation. The same is true for images taken from a natural biological setting, where an expert who is looking for manipulation may be able to see anomalous situations. Metrics that depend on human perception are less precise and are very dependent on the skill and background of the observer, but they have the advantage that they work regardless of format.

When genuinely original images are available, or independently created images of the exact same content (in cases where that is possible), the metrics of manipulation are relatively easy to establish. There are established scales for gradations of light, and for authorial repairs to a slightly damaged image—one with a hair on the lens, for example—that involve a measurable and limited territory on the image. Such situations become more like plagiarism, where the uncertainty does not lie in what or even how much, but in the degree to which the integrity of the research may have been violated.

6.3   DETERMINING FALSIFICATION

Detecting the gray zones is only the first step toward determining falsification. For those who believe in black and white decisions where any copying or manipulation vitiates the work, it is also the only step necessary. This kind of purity sounds attractive but does not belong to the real world of contemporary research, where people must necessarily reuse words and phrases, need to adjust data for extraneous outliers, and have rational arguments for improving the readability of images. The point of grayscale metrics is to establish a continuum where reasonable actions are at one end and intentional deception is at the other. Determining where a particular case falls on the continuum is, however, far from easy.

Plagiarism is the simplest case, because the grayscale is both specific and measurable, but no single scale works for all disciplines because the expectations within the disciplines vary, depending on the degree to which the originality of expressions matters as part of the analysis and the ultimate scholarly or scientific value. Humanists are at one end, the most mathematical and data-driven sciences at the other, and a wealth of social sciences and softer natural sciences occupy the broad middle ground. To a certain degree each discipline must determine where the boundary lies, but it need not be left to mere gut feeling. For plagiarism it should be possible to develop discipline-based expectations based on large-scale comparisons of the existing published literature to establish what quantity of and what kinds of copying, especially copying involving common phrases and structures, have de facto found broad acceptance over the decades. The experiment is quite doable with the right resources and time, and it could help to build better detection tools that recognize specific circumstances and formulations where the reuse of expression is tolerable.

It is equally possible to establish multiple continuums for data where an acceptable degree of manipulation is at one end, and fraud and fabrication are at the other. Data cleaning is a normal operation in most fields, because a certain amount of noise and error is almost inevitable in experimental (and other) settings. If the author will provide a genuinely original version of the data for comparison, a metric can show how much change occurred and how much difference the changes made in the results. One factor is the $p < 0.05$ rule for significance in many social science disciplines ($p < 0.005$ in medicine). Achieving this level of significance often means the difference between reviewers and editors accepting a paper and their rejecting it, even though the boundary itself is arbitrary. That introduces a temptation to look for ways to improve the data just enough to achieve significance, especially if the results are very close. This is not to suggest that legitimate arguments in favor of throwing out or altering some data points should be ignored, or that obviously bad data must be included in analyses; but changes that move results across the significance line probably warrant particular examination.

The biggest problem with data manipulation and falsification lies in getting genuinely original data. An author who intends to deceive can make plausible changes in a supposedly original set of data, with just enough legitimate change to make the set look genuine. The reuse of publicly available data helps to avoid this, even though the providers of such data may also introduce changes, as was seen with the WRDS dataset. The more publicly available data are used in a discipline, the more opportunity exists to compare the characteristics of new datasets with old ones. The risk of accepting existing data sets as reliable is real, but broader comparison options can help to establish plausibility and become a factor in whether to look at data more closely. Data sets have no inherent metadata or standard compression algorithms that help with change detection.

Images in JPEG format have both embedded metadata and compression algorithms that enable change detection, and many biological and medical journals are well on their way to establishing guidelines that use the metrics available from, for example, the forensic droplets. The exact boundary between acceptable manipulation and fraud varies with the journal and the editor, but cutting and pasting images into another image generally crosses the line, while mere cropping generally is acceptable. In the humanities and social sciences, acceptability depends heavily on whether an image is intended to be important evidence for the author's argument, or simply an illustration that might interest the reader, or an expression of the author's original ideas. Essentially anything goes in the last case, and the first is rare enough that very little discussion has taken place. In general cropping and color enhancement are accepted, while inserting, removing, or altering content is unacceptable without a good explanation.

6.4   PREVENTION

A great deal has been written about the role of ethics in prevention, and there is some evidence that ethics training can reduce the instances of plagiarism among undergraduates [Belter and du Pré, 2009]. Training exerts a form of social pressure that is certainly helpful in the short term. It is less clear that similar forms of training make a difference on the less impressionable minds of doctoral students and well-established researchers. This section looks at what steps can be taken to make discovery more certain in order to persuade those who are tempted to violate research integrity that the effort is not worth the risk. This is by no means easy.

Again plagiarism offers the easiest case because relatively good tools are available, and would likely have a chilling effect on plagiarism if publishers used them systematically. The tools cost money, however, and not all publishers make large enough profits that the cost is trivial for them. This is especially a problem for the long tail of very small and open-access publishers, who have no resources for licensing these tools. Checking also costs staff time, or takes the time of editors and reviewers, who may feel that their compensation (if any) does not stretch to analyzing the output of plagiarism checkers or to making decisions about acceptable limits. Nonetheless this is one clear way to discourage plagiarism. A way for large publishers to benefit from their commitment to plagiarism checking might be for them to advertise that all published articles have been checked for plagiarism. Whether that would discourage plagiarism overall remains to be determined.

Preventing data manipulation and falsification is harder. One step is to require researchers to make their data publicly available for inspection and reuse. This means both that a substantial mass of data would be available for comparison and that other researchers could examine the data set for anomalies. A further step would be to require researchers to make the original data available before any cleaning took place. The basic principle is that greater transparency has a discouraging effect on falsification. Those who forge data or manipulate data with an intent to deceive could still do it, but exposing the data would increase the effort they needed to make to create truly plausible data sets.

A further option is to encourage replication of a much larger number of studies. Complete replication (that is, collecting similar new data, not just reusing data from the original study) would have a stronger chance of exposing fake or highly manipulated data. In order to make that feasible, academic researchers would need to get something approaching the level of credit that they would earn for a new experiment. Real equality of credit for a replication may be unlikely, but replication is a good way for younger researchers to learn how to do research. Replication may not appeal to the most ambitious researchers at top universities, but building a market for replication studies may be attractive for those at institutions where research is required but something less than Nobel-prize-level innovation is expected.

Preventing image manipulation and falsification can use elements of the approaches used to prevent both plagiarism and data falsification. If journals systematically used tools such as the ORI makes available for checking, JPEG-based manipulation would likely decline, and the effort required to create undetectable manipulation would increase substantially. Requiring researchers to make their images and original images available would have a similar discouraging effect. And replicating the experiments that produced the images would make exposure very much more likely.

6.5   CONCLUSION

The goal of this chapter and of this lecture is to improve the decision-making about situations where authors may be pushing or actually violating the boundaries of research integrity. Research integrity is no clear and perfect entity that every legitimate scholar recognizes and embraces. It is itself a social construct of methods, ideas, limits, and opportunities that vary from discipline to discipline and to some extent from culture to culture. Research integrity is not a construct that remains stable over time. Research practices that seemed acceptable in the past are not always accepted in the present, nor do the changes always represent additional precision in how we understand integrity. Additional limits intended to close doors to fraud may close them also to unconventional approaches and new ideas. That is the danger of black and white judgments and rigid rules.

A scientist who intentionally altered a JPEG image in order to highlight an undiscovered feature could risk an accusation of fraud under a rule that bans all manipulations, regardless of the reason. Combating fraud is important, but not at the cost of reducing scholarship to simplistic reasoning. Lord Kelvin famously said: "There is nothing new to be discovered in physics now. All that remains is more and more precise measurement" [Weisstein, 2007]. Planck, Bohr, and Einstein soon showed he was wrong, and likewise editors, reviewers, and scholars generally need to remember that the world has not discovered everything necessary to judge plagiarism, data falsification, and image manipulation. Large undiscovered gray zones remain to explore.

The diversity of research is important. While it is often important to look at averages and to estimate a regression line that tells a story about the meaning of the whole dataset, individual data points that stray from the line may nonetheless be worth considering. The same could be true when that data point is a paper that rises into the gray zone of integrity checking without actually representing intentional fraud.

A different mathematical analogy is also appropriate here. Bayesian statistics builds on prior probabilities, and for most authors the prior probability of intentional fraud could be considered zero, whenever no journal has retracted a paper they wrote. Looking more broadly at the actual prior probabilities, however, could change the assessment. For example, an author who has a history of taking expressions from others, even if it does not add up to plagiarism, could be more suspected of future plagiarism than one with no such record. Considering all possible risk factors makes sense as long as it does not become simple prejudice. Some journals automatically treat authors from Asia and Africa as risks for plagiarism and send their papers (and not others) through a plagiarism-checker. This kind of profiling is particularly unfair to researchers at high-quality universities in those areas.

Defining and analyzing the gray zones for research integrity is far from simple. The likelihood is that a nontrivial number of integrity violations remain to be discovered in the existing scholarly literature. If the reader takes away only one point from this book, it should be that our metrics for discovering and determining research integrity violations need continuous development to handle the breadth, subtlety, and flexibility of complex cases.

6.6   HEADT CENTRE

The HEADT Centre[1] has research integrity as one of its core research projects. The HEADT Centre provides active support for universities with complex plagiarism, data falsification, and image manipulation issues. Detection and prevention are part of the goal, but the current focus lies in particular on providing information about the presence of gray zone issues so that subject experts and the appropriate commissions can make informed decisions.

The HEADT Centre offers workshops and training courses, and may well offer certificate programs in the future for those who work with research integrity issues or who are looking for

---

[1]Humboldt Elsevier Advanced Data and Text Centre, <headt.eu>.

positions with universities or publishers that need trained staff for these tasks. Look on the website for more information and future developments.

Research integrity is not a local or a national issue, and international networking among the major players will help to establish best practices, perhaps even de facto standards, for how to discover and judge potential malpractice. At present the decisions and the criteria for these decisions vary from person to person and institution to institution. Those who hunt violations today often have no choice except to take the law into their own hands, because there is no clarity, no formal code, and no formal judges to make a final decision. Building a research integrity network and establishing processes and mechanisms for judgments is part of the HEADT Centre's work.

Bibliography

Abbott, A. (2001). *Chaos of Disciplines.* University of Chicago Press. DOI: 10.7208/chicago/9780226001050.001.0001. 2

"amarcus41" (2012-11-20). Accounting fraud paper retracted for "misstatement." http://retractionwatch.com/2012/11/20/accounting-fraud-paper-retracted-for-misstatement/ 59

(Pseudonym) ASC, P. (2011-05-25). *Illness, Media, and Culture—Ein Interkultureller Vergleich der Darstellung von Allergien in Englischen und US-amerikanischen Lifestyle-Magazinen.* Humboldt-Universität zu Berlin. http://edoc.hu-berlin.de/docviews/abstract.php?lang=ger&id=38099 25

Ascherson, N. (2010a). "Liquidator." Rev. of hugh trevor-roper: The biography, by Adam Sisman. *London Review of Books*, 32(16), pages 10–12. http://www.lrb.co.uk/v32/n16/neal-ascherson/liquidator 48

Ascherson, N. (2010b). "Liquidator." Rev. of hugh trevor-roper: The biography, by Adam Sisman. *London Review of Books*, 32(16), pages 10–12. http://www.lrb.co.uk/v32/n16/neal-ascherson/liquidator 48

Bamber, L. S., Christensen, T. E., and Gaver, K. M. (2000). Do we really "know" what we think we know? A case study of seminal research and its subsequent overgeneralization. *Accounting, Organizations and Society* 25(2), pages 103–129. DOI: 10.2139/ssrn.208628. 88

Beck, T. S. (2016). *Shaping Images: Scholarly Perspectives on Image Manipulation.* DeGruyter. ISBN 978-3-11-047709-2. DOI: 10.1515/9783110477092. 3, 90

Becker-Dillingen, J. (1929). *Handbuch des Gesamten Pflanzenbaues Einschliesslich der Pflanzenzüchtung: Bd. Handbuch des Hülsenfruchtbaues und Futerbaues.* Handbuch des gesamten pflanzenbaues einschliesslich der pflanzenzüchtung. P. Parey. https://books.google.de/books?id=kkMLAQAAIAAJ 39

Belter, R. W. and du Pré, A. (2009). A strategy to reduce plagiarism in an undergraduate course. *Teaching of Psychology*, 36(4), pages 257–261. http://www.tandfonline.com/doi/abs/10.1080/00986280903173165 DOI: 10.1080/00986280903173165. 106

Bhattacharjee, Y. (2013, apr). Diederik Stapel's Audacious Academic Fraud. http://www.ny times.com/2013/04/28/magazine/diederik-stapels-audacious-academic-fraud. html?pagewanted=allhttp://www.nytimes.com/2013/04/28/magazine/diederik-stapels-audacious-academic-fraud.html?pagewanted=all{&}{_}r=1 56, 57

Blinkhorm, S. F. (1989). Was burt stitched up? *Nature*, (340), pages 439–440. DOI: 10.1038/340439a0. 53

Bors, D. A. and MacLeod, C. M. (1996). *Memory*. Elsevier. ISBN 978-0-12-102570-0. http://www.sciencedirect.com/science/article/pii/B9780121025700500148 7

Bredekamp, H. (2007). Galilei der künstler: Der mond. *Die Sonne. Die Hand*, 2. 50

Brückle, I. and Hahn, O. (2011). *Galileo's Sidereus Nuncius: A Comparison of the Proof Copy (New York) with Other Paradigmatic Copies*. Akademie Verlag. 50

Budd, J. (2013). The stapel case: An object lesson in research integrity and its lapses. *Synesis: A Journal of Science, Technology, Ethics, and Policy* 4(1), pages G47–G53. 53

Budd, J., Coble, Z., and Abritis, A. (2016). An investigation of retracted articles in the biomedical literature. *Proc. of the 79th ASS&T Annual Meeting*, 53. 53

Burgess, S. (1998). GIMP—A brief (and ancient) history of GIMP. //www.gimp.org/about /ancient_history.html 76

Call, A., Hewitt, M., Watkins, J., and Yohn, T. L. (2016-06-03). Changes in the i/b/e/s database and their effect on the observed properties of analyst forecasts. http://papers.ssrn.com/sol3/papers.cfm?abstract_id=2788140 62

Camerer, C. F., Dreber, A., Forsell, E., Ho, T.-H., Huber, J., Johannesson, M., Kirchler, M., Almenberg, J., Altmejd, A., Chan, T., et al. (2016). Evaluating replicability of laboratory experiments in economics. 351(6280), pages 1433–1436. http://science.sciencemag.org/content/351/6280/1433.abstract DOI: 10.1126/science.aaf0918. 13, 54, 55, 56

Canon Europe, (2016). CCD and CMOS sensors. http://cpn.canon-europe.com/content/education/infobank/capturing_the_image/ccd_and_cmos_sensors.do 77

Castelvecchi, D. (2015-05-15). Physics paper sets record with more than 5,000 authors. http://www.nature.com/doifinder/10.1038/nature.2015.17567 DOI: 10.1038/nature.2015.17567. 36

Cell Press (2016). Information for authors: Cell. http://www.cell.com/cell/authors 94

Chawla, D. S. (2016-07-12). Cardiology retractions archives. http://retractionwatch.com/category/by-subject/clinical-study-retractions/cardiology-retractions/ 92, 95

Crocker, J. (2011). The road to fraud starts with a single step. *Nature*, 479(7372), page 151. `http: //www.nature.com/news/2011/111109/full/479151a.html` DOI: 10.1038/479151a. 6

Davis, M., Davis, K. J., and Dunagan, M. M. (2012). *Scientific Papers and Presentations*. Elsevier. ISBN 978-0-12-384727-0. `http://www.sciencedirect.com/science/article/pii/B9780123847270000124` 8

Eklund, A., Nichols, T. E., and Knutsson, H. (2016). Cluster failure: Why fmri inferences for spatial extent have inflated false-positive rates. *Proc. of the National Academy of Sciences*, 201602413. DOI: 10.1073/pnas.1602413113. 97

Enserink, M. (2012). Fraud-detection tool could shake up psychology. *Science* 337(6090), pages 21–22. `http://science.sciencemag.org/content/337/6090/21.full` DOI: 10.1126/science.337.6090.21. 12, 58

Fear, K. (2013). Measuring and anticipating the impact of data reuse. `https: //deepblue.lib.umich.edu/bitstream/handle/2027.42/102481/kfear_1.pdf? sequence=1&isAllowed=y` 45

Feist, (1991). Feist publications, inc. v. rural telephone service co., 499 U.S. 340. `https://www. law.cornell.edu/copyright/cases/499_US_340.htm` 43

Ferguson, C. (2014-11-06). University of Utah investigation fingers chem engineering grad student for misconduct. `http://retractionwatch.com/2014/11/06/university-of-utah-investigation-fingers-chemistry-grad-student-for-misconduct/` 98

Fischer, B. (2016-02-19). Schwerin—Plagiatsjäger: Backhaus hat in doktorarbeit abgekupfert. `http://www.ostsee-zeitung.de/Nachrichten/MV-aktuell/Politik/Plagiatsjaeger-Backhaus-hat-in-Doktorarbeit-abgekupfert` 36, 37

Ford, M. (2016-08). I gotta use words: Eliot speaks in tongues. 38(16), pages 9–12. `http: //www.lrb.co.uk/v38/n16/mark-ford/i-gotta-use-words` 103

Fox, M. (2015-01-07). Lee Israel, a writer proudest of her literary forgeries, dies at 75—The New York Times. `http://www.nytimes.com/2015/01/08/arts/lee-israel-a-writer-proudest-of-her-literary-forgeries-dies-at-75.html?_r=1` 52, 53

Furman, J. L., Jensen, K., and Murray, F. (2012). Governing knowledge in the scientific community: Exploring the role of retractions in biomedicine. *Research Policy* 41(2), pages 276–290. `http://www.sciencedirect.com/science/article/pii/S0048733311002174` `http: //www.sciencedirect.com/science/article/pii/S0048733311002174/pdfft?md5= 3d76d731feeafd5864c01d1c02dc0342{&}pid=1-s2.0-S0048733311002174-main.pdf` DOI: 10.1016/j.respol.2011.11.001. 64

Glassner, L. and Dixon, W. (1986-03-27). Oral history of Wilfrid Dixon and Linda Glassner. http://www.computerhistory.org/collections/catalog/102658169 87

Glater, J. D. (2005-03-03). Martha Stewart gets new body in newsweek. http://www.nytimes.com/2005/03/03/business/media/martha-stewart-gets-new-body-in-newsweek.html 83

Golus, C. (2016). What do you know? http://mag.uchicago.edu/university-news/what-do-you-know?msource=SHORTLIST&tr=y&auid=16862052 98

Grant, J. (1985). The Diaries of Adolf Hitler. *Journal of the Forensic Science Society* 25(3), page 189. http://www.sciencedirect.com/science/article/pii/S0015736885723912 DOI: 10.1016/s0015-7368(85)72391-2. 48

Gunnarsson, J., Kulesza, W. J., and Pettersson, A. (2014-05). Teaching international students how to avoid plagiarism: Librarians and faculty in collaboration. 40(3), pages 413–417. http://www.sciencedirect.com/science/article/pii/S0099133314000603 DOI: 10.1016/j.acalib.2014.04.006. 8

GuttenPlag-Anonymous (2011). GuttenPlag wiki. http://de.guttenplag.wikia.com/wiki/GuttenPlag_Wiki 34

Healy, B. (2012-12-21). Bentley accounting professor James Hunton, amid controversy over retraction, resigns—The Boston Globe. https://www.bostonglobe.com/business/2012/12/21/bentley-accounting-professor-james-hunton-amid-controversy-over-retraction-resigns/y4JtNvlr1SwNnFcpBFcY4J/story.html 59

Hein, J., Zobrist, R., Konrad, C., and Schuepfer, G. (2012). Scientific fraud in 20 falsified anesthesia papers. *Der Anaesthesist* 61(6), pages 543–549. DOI: 10.1007/s00101-012-2029-x. 67

Hunton, J. E. and Gold, A. (2012-11-09). Retraction: A field experiment comparing the outcomes of three fraud brainstorming procedures: Nominal group, round robin, and open discussion. 88(1), pages 357–357. http://aaajournals.org/doi/abs/10.2308/accr-10326 DOI: 10.2308/accr-10326. 60

Indiana University (2011-08-11). Examples of plagiarism, and of appropriate use of others' words and ideas. http://www.indiana.edu/~wts/pamphlets/plagiarism.pdf 23

Janson, J. (2016). Han van Meegeren's fake vermeers. http://www.essentialvermeer.com/misc/van_meegeren.html#.V9VZ2ph97s2 51

Johnson, C. Y. (2014-05-30). Internal Harvard report shines light on misconduct by star psychology researcher, Marc Hauser. https://www.bostonglobe.com/metro/2014/

05/29/internal-harvard-report-shines-light-misconduct-star-psychology-researcher-marc-hauser/maSUowPqL4clXrOgj44aKP/story.html 71, 72

Joynson, R. B. (1989). *The Burt affair.* Florence, KY, Taylor and Frances/Routledge. (Hardcover). DOI: 10.1111/j.2044-8279.1990.tb00954.x. 53

Kakuk, P. (2009). The legacy of the hwang case: Research misconduct in biosciences. *Science and Engineering Ethics* 15(4), pages 545–562. DOI: 10.1007/s11948-009-9121-x. 66, 67

Klovert, H. (2015-10-02). Plagiatsjaeger im netz: Wer steckt hinter VroniPlag? http://www.spiegel.de/unispiegel/studium/plagiate-in-doktorarbeiten-wer-sind-die-plagiatsjaeger-a-1055760.html 25

Landreth, K. (2016). RAW photos with GIMP | how to GIMP. http://howtogimp.com/raw-photos-with-gimp/ 79

Lee, Y. (2011-01). Understanding anti-plagiarism software adoption: An extended protection motivation theory perspective. 50(2), pages 361–369. http://www.sciencedirect.com/science/article/pii/S0167923610001156 DOI: 10.1016/j.dss.2010.07.009. 7, 9

Maiväli, Ü. (2015). Chapter 1—Do we need a science of science? pages 3–53. Academic Press, Boston. http://www.sciencedirect.com/science/article/pii/B9780124186897000016 65, 66

Malone, J. (2014-07-21). Report of Judith A. Malone, Bentley University ethics officer, concerning Dr. James E. Hunton. https://www.bentley.edu/files/Hunton%20report%20July21.pdf 59, 60

McCook, A. (2015-09-29). German department head reprimanded for not catching mistakes of co-author lichtenthaler. http://retractionwatch.com/2015/09/29/german-department-head-reprimanded-for-not-catching-mistakes-of-co-author/ 71

McFadden, R. D. (1983, Apr 23). Skepticism growing over the "Hitler Diaries." http://www.nytimes.com/1983/04/25/world/skepticism-growing-over-the-hitler-diaries.html 48

McGrane, S. (2013). Diary of the Hitler hoax. http://www.newyorker.com/books/page-turner/diary-of-the-hitler-diary-hoax 48

National Science Foundation (2000). Visualization—A way to the unseen. http://nsf.gov/about/history/nsf0050/visualization/pdf.htm 86

Newman, A. (2013, nov). The art of detecting data and image manipulation. http://editorsupdate.elsevier.com/issue-41-november-2013/the-art-of-detecting-data-and-image-manipulation/ 12

Department of Commerce NIST, (2013-10-30). NIST/SEMATECH e-handbook of statistical methods. `http://www.itl.nist.gov/div898/handbook/index.htm` 70

Oberg, J. (2013). Cosmonauts who weren't there. In *Cold War Space Sleuths*, pages 87–110. Springer. DOI: 10.1007/978-1-4614-3052-0_4. 82

U.S. Office of Research Integrity, (2000). Policies—ORI mission | ORI—The office of research integrity. `http://ori.hhs.gov/ori-mission` 93

Office of Research Integrity (2012-07-24a). Droplets | ORI—The office of research integrity. `https://ori.hhs.gov/droplets` 99

Office of Research Integrity (2012-07-24b). Forensic actions | ORI—The office of research integrity. `https://ori.hhs.gov/actions` 99, 100

Office of Research Integrity (2014-11-06). Policies—ORI mission | ORI—The office of research integrity. `https://ori.hhs.gov/ori-mission` 40

Office of Research Integrity (2016). Case summaries | ORI—The office of research integrity. `https://ori.hhs.gov/case_summary` 66

Office of Research Integrity (2016-05-24). Case summary: Malhotra, Ricky | ORI—The office of research integrity. `http://ori.hhs.gov/content/case-summary-malhotra-ricky` 95

Office of Research Integrity (2016-07-20). Case summary: Li, Zhiyu | ORI—The office of research integrity. `https://ori.hhs.gov/content/case-summary-li-zhiyu` 91, 92

Oltermann, P. (2016). Human-animal studies academics dogged by German hoaxers. `https://www.theguardian.com/world/2016/mar/01/human-animal-studies-academics-dogged-by-german-hoaxers` 46

Oppenheimer, D. M., Meyvis, T., and Davidenko, N. (2009). Instructional manipulation checks: Detecting satisficing to increase statistical power. *Journal of Experimental Social Psychology* 45(4), pages 867–872. `http://www.sciencedirect.com/science/article/pii/S0022103109000766` DOI: 10.1016/j.jesp.2009.03.009. 62

Oransky, I. (2012-07-17). Three papers by German management professor retracted for duplication, statistical issues. `http://retractionwatch.com/2012/07/17/three-papers-by-german-management-prof-retracted-for-duplication-statistical-issues/` 71

Ostsee Zeitung anonymous writer (2016). Zusammenfassung_dissertationspruefung.pdf. `https://docs.google.com/viewer?url=http%3A%2F%2Fcdn-media.ln-und-oz.de%2Fmedien%2FDissertationspr%25C3%25BCfung_Till_Backhaus%2FZusammenfassung_Dissertationspr%25C3%25BCfung.pdf` 37

Palus, S. (2016-03-29). Concerns about image manipulation? Sorry, the data were lost in a flood. http://retractionwatch.com/2016/03/29/concerns-about-image-manipulation-sorry-the-data-were-lost-in-a-flood/ 93, 96

Palus, S. (2016-05-19). Software glitch—not intentional manipulation—sunk immunology paper, says author. http://retractionwatch.com/2016/05/19/software-glitch-not-intentional-manipulation-sunk-immunology-paper/ 98

Ploth, D. W. (2014-10). Ethics in publishing—today's epidemic. 348(4), pages 269–70. http://www.sciencedirect.com/science/article/pii/S0002962915302068 5

Plotz, D. (2002). The Plagiarist. *Slate.com*. 31. http://www.slate.com/id/2060618/. AccessedJanuary 20

Princeton University (2016). Examples of plagiarism—academic integrity at Princeton University. https://www.princeton.edu/pr/pub/integrity/pages/plagiarism/ 21, 22

re3data (2016-04-13). re3data.org reaches a milestone and begins offering badges. http://www.re3data.org/ 46

Reich, E. S. (2009). The rise and fall of a physics fraudster. *Physics World* 22(5), pages 24–29. http://iopscience.iop.org/article/10.1088/2058-7058/22/05/37/pdf DOI: 10.1088/2058-7058/22/05/37. 64, 65

Schmidle, N. (2013). A very rare book: The mystery surrounding a copy of Galileo's pivotal treatise. *New Yorker* December 1. http://www.newyorker.com/magazine/2013/12/16/a-very-rare-book 49, 50, 51

Schneider, C. A., Rasband, W. S., and Eliceiri, K. W. (2012-07-01). NIH image to ImageJ: 25 years of image analysis. 9(7), pages 671–675. http://www.nature.com/nmeth/journal/v9/n7/full/nmeth.2089.html 97

Sexy23-anonymous (2016). sexy23 bookmarks. http://sci.sexy23.de/section/wtf/ 31

Shapin, S. (2010). Lowering the tone in the history of science. In *Never Pure: Historical Studies of Science as if it was Produced by People with Bodies, Situated in Time, Space, Culture, and Society, and Struggling for Credibility and Authority*, pages 4–14. Johns Hopkins Press. xvii

Shaw, J. (2001-08-05). Derek Freeman, who challenged Margaret Mead on Samoa, dies at 84. http://www.nytimes.com/2001/08/05/world/derek-freeman-who-challenged-margaret-mead-on-samoa-dies-at-84.html 52

Shewan, L. G. and Coats, A. J. S. (2010, sep). Ethics in the authorship and publishing of scientific articles. *International Journal of Cardiology* 144(1), pages 1–2. http://www.sciencedirect.com/science/article/pii/S0167527310005577 http:

//www.sciencedirect.com/science/article/pii/S0167527310005577/pdfft?md5=
ad78dc486ff81a633db02fa0919f5058{&}pid=1-s2.0-S0167527310005577-main.pdf
DOI: 10.1016/j.ijcard.2010.07.030. 7

Silver, N. (2016-06-29). A user's guide to FiveThirtyEight's 2016 general election
forecast. http://fivethirtyeight.com/features/a-users-guide-to-fivethirtyei
ghts-2016-general-election-forecast/ 63

Simonsohn, U. (2013). Just post it the lesson from two cases of fabricated data detected by statistics alone. *Psychological science*, page 0956797613480366. http://pss.sagepub.com/conten
t/early/2013/08/23/0956797613480366.abstract DOI: 10.1177/0956797613480366.
12, 13

Simonsohn, U. (2014). Just post it: The lesson from two cases of fabricated data detected by
statistics alone. *Psychological Science*, pages 1–31. http://pss.sagepub.com/content/earl
y/2013/08/23/0956797613480366.abstract DOI: 10.1177/0956797613480366. 58, 59

Sontag, S. (1977). *On Photography*. Penguin. DOI: 10.1080/10948007809488930. 3

Stamm, M. C. and Liu, K. J. R. (2010). Forensic detection of image manipulation using statistical
intrinsic fingerprints. 5(3), pages 492–506. http://sig.umd.edu/publications/Stamm_T
IFS_201009.pdf DOI: 10.1109/tifs.2010.2053202. 80

Stapel, D. A. and Lindenberg, S. (2011). Coping with chaos: How disordered contexts promote
stereotyping and discrimination. 332(6026), pages 251–253. http://science.sciencemag
.org/content/332/6026/251.full DOI: 10.1126/science.1201068. 57, 58

Stroupe, C. (2004). The rhetoric of irritation: Inappropriateness as visual/literate practice. In
Defining Visual Rhetorics, pages 243–258. Routledge. 82

TB (2001). *BackhausDiss_inkl_Kommentare_und_Linien.pdf*. https://docs.google.com/vi
ewer?url=http%3A%2F%2Fcdn-media.ln-und-oz.de%2Fmedien%2FDissertationspr%
25C3%25BCfung_Till_Backhaus%2FBackhausDiss_inkl_Kommentare_und_Linien.pdf
39, 40

Teledyne, (2016). CCD vs. CMOS—teledyne DALSA inc. https://www.teledynedalsa.co
m/imaging/knowledge-center/appnotes/ccd-vs-cmos/ 77

Van Noorden, R. (2015-06-12). The image detective who roots out manuscript
flaws. http://www.nature.com/news/the-image-detective-who-roots-out-manusc
ript-flaws-1.17749 DOI: 10.1038/nature.2015.17749. 101

Vroniplag, W. (2016). Vroniplag introduction. http://de.vroniplag.wikia.com/wiki/Home
25, 28

Weber-Wulff, D. (2015). Response to Diane Pecorari's "plagiarism in second language writing: Is it time to close the case?". 30, pages 103–104. http://www.sciencedirect.com/scienc e/article/pii/S1060374315000594 DOI: 10.1016/j.jslw.2015.08.005. 6

Weber-Wulff, D., Möller, C., Touras, J., and Zincke, E. (2015). Plagiarism detection software test 2013. http://plagiat.htw-berlin.de/wp-content/uploads/Testbericht-2013-color.pdf 10, 11

Weisstein, E. W. (2007). Kelvin, Lord William Thomson (1824–1907)—from Eric Weisstein's world of scientific biography. http://scienceworld.wolfram.com/biography/Kelvin.html 108

Wickham, H. (2012-01-01). A layered grammar of graphics. http://www.tandfonline.com/doi/abs/10.1198/jcgs.2009.07098 DOI: 10.1198/jcgs.2009.07098. 87

Wikipedia (2016-07-29). Western blot. Page version ID: 732125088. https://en.wikipedia.org/w/index.php?title=Western_blot&oldid=732125088 95

WIPO, (1997). Germany: Federal act establishing the general conditions for information and communication services (information and communication services act). http://www.wipo.int/wipolex/en/text.jsp?file_id=126233 43

Wollny, E. (1896). Untersuchungen über das verhalten der atmosphärischen niederschläge zur pflanze und zum boden. VI, pages 380–385. http://bibdigital.rjb.csic.es/ing/Libro.php?Libro=3205 39

World Press Photo (2016a). World press photo—about. http://www.worldpressphoto.org/about 84

World Press Photo (2016b). Photo contest entry rules. http://www.worldpressphoto.org/activities/photo-contest/entry-rules 83

Zeldin, T. (1979). *France 1848–1945: Ambition and Love.* Oxford University Press. 2

Zirm, J. (2008-10-30). Der tucholsky-schwindel. http://diepresse.com/home/wirtschaft/finanzkrise/426781/Der-TucholskySchwindel 53

Author's Biography

MICHAEL SEADLE

Michael Seadle is a professor at Humboldt-Universität zu Berlin, and is the chair of the Commission on Research Malpractice.[2] His experience with research integrity issues builds in part on over 20 years of experience as a journal editor, where he confronted plagiarism and other research integrity issues. As dean he also dealt with such issues at the bachelor's and master's level. When Elsevier approached him to fund a research project, he suggested research integrity. This led to the establishment of the HEADT Centre (Humboldt-Elsevier Advanced Data and Text Centre), whose mission is in part to investigate research integrity issues.

His background blends multiple fields. Early in his university career Seadle studied chemistry, but discovered that he did not like the lab work and spent his time working on computing issues. After studying in Vienna, he switched to history, and completed a doctorate in that discipline at the University of Chicago under the supervision of William H. McNeill. He returned then to computing, and worked for years in industry before making his way back to the academic world at Cornell and Michigan State University. In 2006 he was called to Berlin to strengthen the research reputation of the Berlin School of Library and Information Science (Institut für Bibliotheks- und Informationswissenschaft at Humboldt-Universität zu Berlin). In Berlin he has served as chair of the international iSchools group, and has received multiple grants from the German Research Society (Deutsche Forschungsgemeinschaft), particularly in the area of long-term digital archiving. At the university he has been director of the School, dean of the Fakultät, and chair of the University Council.

---

[2]Kommission zur Überprüfung von Vorwürfen wissenschaftlichen Fehlverhaltens.

Printed in the United States
by Baker & Taylor Publisher Services